STYLE AND STRATEGY
OF THE BUSINESS LETTER

Jacqueline Trace

*State University of New York
at Fredonia*

Prentice-Hall, Inc., Englewood Cliffs, New Jersey 07632

Library of Congress Cataloging in Publication Data

Trace, Jacqueline.
  Style and strategy of the business letter.

Includes index.
  1. Commercial correspondence. I. Title.
HF5721.T72 1985   808'.066651   84-24992
ISBN 0–13–858895–3
ISBN 0–13–858887–2 (pbk.)

Editorial/production supervision and
   interior design: Fred Dahl
Cover design: George Cornell
Manufacturing buyer: Edward O'Dougherty

Printed in the United States of America

10 9 8 7 6 5 4 3 2 1

ISBN 0-13-858895-3   01

ISBN 0-13-858887-2 {PBK.}   01

Prentice-Hall International, Inc., *London*
Prentice-Hall of Australia Pty. Limited, *Sydney*
Editora Prentice-Hall do Brasil, Ltda., *Rio de Janeiro*
Prentice-Hall Canada Inc., *Toronto*
Prentice-Hall Hispanoamericana, S.A., *Mexico*
Prentice-Hall of India Private Limited, *New Delhi*
Prentice-Hall of Japan, Inc., *Tokyo*
Prentice-Hall of Southeast Asia Pte. Ltd., *Singapore*
Whitehall Books Limited, *Wellington, New Zealand*

CONTENTS

List of Illustrations, ix
Preface, xi
Acknowledgments, xiii

PART ONE
LAYING OUT THE LETTER
TO LOOK PROFESSIONAL AND GAIN ATTENTION
1
Format, 1
   Margins, 3
   Heading, 3
   Dateline, 5
   Special Notations, 6
   "Personal and Confidential" Notation, 6
   Inside Address, 7
      Courtesy Titles, 8
      Organizational Titles, 9
      Company Name, 10
      Street Address, 11
      City, State, and Zip Code, 11
   Attention Line, 11
   Subject Line, 13
   Salutation, 14
   Your Message, 16
   Complimentary Close, 17

Your Name and Organizational Title, 17
Reference Initials, 18
Enclosure Line, 19
Copy Notation, 20
Postscript, 21
Second Page, 22
The Envelope, 22

PART TWO

PLANNING YOUR STRATEGY TO INVOLVE THE READER

2
Message, 24

Purpose, 26
Audience, 26
The Right Beginning, 27
     Use the Direct Style for Most Letters, 28
     Lead into a Negative or Unexpected Message, 28
Tone, 28
     Be Positive, 28
     Adopt the Reader's Point of View, 30
Length, 32

3
The Letter of Request, 34

Use the Direct Approach, 34
Explain Your Problem, 35
Express Appreciation, 37

4
The Letter of Complaint, 40

Keep Cool, 41
Write to the Right Person, 41
Show Them You Mean Business, 42
Summarize the Problem and Your Position, 44
Present the Background Details, 44
Ask for an Adjustment, 45

5

The Letter of Refusal, 48

Open with a Positive Statement to Establish Empathy, 49
Disclose the Background Information, 49
State the Refusal, 50
Present Alternatives or Offer Suggestions, 50
Close on a Friendly Note, 50
Avoid Negative Words, 51

6

The Letter of Persuasion, 57

A Community-Based Project, 57
 Work up Some Enthusiasm for Your Project, 58
 Discover and Create Some Reader Motives, 58
 Attract Attention, 60
  Get the Reader Involved, 60
  Establish a Common Bond Between You and Your Reader, 65
 Build an argument, 66
  Describe Fully the Ideas Behind Your Cause, 66
  Slowly Reveal the Purpose of the Letter, 67
  Provide Testimonials, 68
  Use Knowledge to Build Feelings, 69
 Ask for Action, 70
 Keep the Typography Simple, 71
A Letter to a Politician, 72
 Come Across as a Real Person, 73
 Follow the 3A's, 73
 Get to the Point Quickly, 76
 Exhibit Your Knowledge, 76
 Be Assertive, 76
 End with Power, 77
 Get Extra Mileage from the Carbon Copy, 78

7

The Resume and Letter of Application, 79

The Blind Approach, 80
The Informed Approach, 82
 Research the Job and the Organization, 82
 Research Yourself, 84
Resume Basics, 84
 Make It Letter Perfect, 84
 Keep It on One Page, 85

The Reverse Chronological Resume, 87
  Type Your Name, Address and Phone Number First, 89
  Follow It with Your Work History, 89
  List Your Educational Qualifications Next, 91
  Mention Other Relevant Activities or Awards, 91
A Letter to Accompany the Reverse Chronological Resume, 94
  Capture the Reader's Attention in the First Paragraph, 95
  Show That You Can Do the Job, 96
  Offer to Provide References, 98
  Omit Reference to Your Salary Expectations, 98
  Ask for an Interview, 98
  Send it Early, 99
The Functional Resume, 99
  Categorize Your Qualifications by Function, 101
  Don't Restrict Your Skills to Employment Functions, 103
  Use Bullets to Set Off Each Function, 104
  Briefly Outline Your Work History, 104
  Place Your Educational Degree(s) Last, 104
A Letter to Accompany the Functional Resume, 105

PART THREE

EDITING YOUR LETTER TO HOLD THE READER'S INTEREST

8
Style, 109

The Word, 109
  Choose the Plain Word over the Fancy, 109
  Make Your Verbs Strong, 111
  Remove Redundant Words, 114
  Wipe out Prepositional Deadwood, 116
  Abandon Needless Pronouns, 117
  Eliminate Unnecessary That's, *118*
  Don't Leave This *in a Vacuum, 120*
  Use It *(Not* They) *for Collective Nouns, 121*
The Sentence, 122
  Avoid "Dick and Jane" Sentences, 122
  If an Idea Is Important, Give It a Sentence of Its own, 125
  Keep the Parts of Your Sentence in the Right Order, 127
  Don't Dangle the Modifiers, 129
  Set Up Sequences of Ideas in Parallel Form, 131
  Make Your Numbers Visible, 135
  Underline to Emphasize Ideas, 136
  Don't Interrupt Sentence Flow by Awkward Word Division, 137

The Paragraph, 138
    Shun Long Paragraphs, 138
    Consider the One-sentence Paragraph, 141
    List Ideas Vertically to Create White Space, 142
    Link Up Ideas with Transition Words, 143
Modern Business Style, 144
    Abandon Business Cliches, 144
    Adopt Specific, Concrete Words, 146
    Watch the Spelling of These Commonly Confused Words, 147
    Sprinkle Your Prose with Contractions for the Right Rhythm, 155
    Don't Be Afraid to Address Your Reader by Name, 156
    Eliminate Sexist Words from Your Vocabulary, 157

APPENDIX A
Recommended Forms of Address for Government
Officials and Other Professionals, 159

APPENDIX B
Common Business Abbreviations, 165

Index, 172

LIST OF
ILLUSTRATIONS

Figure 1–1   An Average-Length Letter in Full-Block Style, 4

Figure 1–2   Envelope Format, 23

Model No. 1   Letter of Request, 36

Model No. 2   Letter of Request, 38

Model No. 3   Letter of Complaint, 43

Model No. 4   Letter of Complaint, 46

Model No. 5   Letter of Refusal, 52

Model No. 6   Letter of Refusal, 55

Model No. 7   Letter of Persuasion, 61

Model No. 8   Letter of Persuasion, 74

Model No. 9   Reverse Chronological Resume, 88

Model No. 10 Letter of Application, 97

Model No. 11 Functional Resume, 102

Model No. 12 Letter of Application, 106

Table 1–1   State Abbreviations for Use with ZIP Codes, 12

PREFACE

This little book is written for all those people—young and old, rich and poor, unskilled and professional, employed and unemployed—who want to improve their lives by making business letters work for them. Whether this is your introduction to the mysteries of the formal letter or an attempt to bring yourself up to date with the latest customs in business writing, you will find that you can increase control over the daily events of your life by following the principles laid out in this book.

Some of these rules may seem arbitrary—and they are. Traditions die hard, and you will have to master some writing practices that are, in fact, nothing more than arbitrary conventions. But once you have mastered these conventions, exciting challenges begin, and you will be faced with tasks that demand creativity, discretion, good judgment, and a respect for humanity.

If you have your own secretary, you may wish to skip by the format principles outlined in the first chapter. On the other hand, you may not. Times change, and letter format practices change with them. Even your secretary may be unaware of acceptable contemporary usage in letter construction.

Consideration of the reader's needs and how best to satisfy them—as well as your own needs to get what you want—is the subject of Chapters 2 through 7. Many letters fail because business writers refuse to accept the challenge posed by their problems. By viewing every letter-writing assignment as a problem to be solved, you will learn how to carefully plan your message to persuade the reader to understand and accept your point of view. These chapters on strategy examine organization, tone, and empathy.

Finally, in Chapter 8 you will learn how to make your language interesting to hold the reader's attention. An understanding of sentence and paragraph style, visual techniques of presentation, and word choice all serve to keep the reader alert to your message.

These basic principles of style and strategy are illustrated through the pen of Robin Redgrave, as she moves from New York to Texas, manages a business, coordinates a fund drive, and looks for employment.

I hope you will enjoy her story.

JACQUELINE TRACE

ACKNOWLEDGMENTS

I wish to thank Robert Schweik, Distinguished Teaching Professor at the State University College at Fredonia, and my former student, Mary P. Sundeen, for their useful editorial comments and suggestions. My appreciation extends also to Professor Douglas Shepard for helping me proofread this book. Finally, I am grateful to my students at Fredonia, who helped me put into perspective many of the principles discussed here; to my children, Cassandra and Thomas Trace, for their support during the months this book was being written; and to Audrey J. Miga for typing the manuscript.

CHAPTER **1**

FORMAT

THE FIRST REQUIREMENT of any business letter, something your readers expect to see before they read the letter, is a professional *look*. Every business letter creates an instant impression in the mind of its reader by its overall appearance on the page. If a letter is handwritten or sloppily typed, you can destroy your credibility in an instant. No one, businessperson or consumer, will be receptive to the ideas of someone who hasn't taken the time to present those ideas in an attractive way. If you want your letter to bring results, it must be carefully designed.

Whether you type your own letter or have someone type it for you, give it good visibility on the page by making sure you have a fresh ribbon in the typewriter. Readability is the key to all good writing, and no piece of writing is readable unless you can see the words. The visual appearance of your letter will be enhanced, therefore, by using a standard pica typeface rather than the smaller elite or script type. When the words are bigger, the ideas stand out better.

It will be to your advantage, especially in a very important letter, to compose a draft, or trial run, before typing the final copy. Very few people, and only those who have had long experience at it, can sit down and type or dictate an effective, well organized letter the first time around.

Writing is a three-step process. First you plan, then you write, then you revise. The planning stage, covered in Chapters 2 through

7, involves thinking through your strategy: What are you trying to achieve by your letter? What is the best way to go about it? Once you have determined this strategy you can begin to put words down on paper.

The process does not stop there. You will then need to reexamine those words to ensure they are organized logically and presented clearly. In this final, revising stage, you will want to examine every paragraph, sentence, and word to make sure your message will be interpreted correctly. You will also need to check with a good dictionary, so that no misspellings detract from your credibility as a writer.* Only then is your letter ready to send out.

If you want your ideas to work for you, accept this three-step method. Draft your letter before you type it.

You may handwrite or type your first draft. Most people, excluding professional writers, are less inhibited when they think with pen or pencil. If you are one of these people, compose your first draft on lined paper. On the other hand, if you are agile and comfortable at a typewriter, or if your handwriting is sloppy, you may find it easier to mark up and work from a typewritten page. Moreover, a rough draft that is typed will give you a better idea of how the letter will space out on the page, so that the second time around the letter will be ready to sign. If you have any experience at all with typewriters, try this method. You may be able to save some time in the long run.

When you are ready to type your final copy, start with a letterhead or piece of plain white paper of the standard 8½×11″ size. Colored paper may give an unbusinesslike impression. Worse yet is stationery with floral designs running through the entire page. Regular bond paper is preferable to the erasable type, which smudges easily on contact with a ballpoint pen or sweaty palm. Though type is harder to erase on a good bond paper, a "white out" correction fluid will do the job neatly.

One further warning: Use onionskin, which is thin, transparent paper, only for your carbon copies, not for the original letter. In other words, don't do anything to distract your reader from your message, which you want to come through loud and clear.

Buy a box of carbon paper and some onionskin, so that you can make carbon copies of all your correspondence. Never send anything

---

*I recommend *Webster's New World Dictionary of the American Language* (Englewood Cliffs, N.J.: Prentice-Hall, Inc., 1976) and *The American Heritage Dictionary of the English Language* (Boston: Houghton Mifflin Company, 1982).

through the mail without keeping a copy for yourself. You may need proof later of when you sent your letter and exactly what you said. Hold on to the evidence.

With a rough draft in front of you and your paper in the typewriter, you are ready to go. Many letter formats are available to the professional letter writer. Most common today, however, is the full-block style. It is preferable to other styles because it is easiest on the typist. The full-block format is explained on the following pages and used for all the letters in this book. (See Figure 1–1 for an illustration of the layout of an average-length letter in full-block style.)

MARGINS

If your letter is of average length (two to four paragraphs), set margins of 15 spaces on each side. For longer letters you will need to use 10-space margins so that you can get the whole letter on one page. Very short letters of two or three sentences call for wide margins of 20 spaces at the right and left.

You should double space your message only in brief letters comprising two or three sentences. Letters of normal length should always be single-spaced, with double spaces between paragraphs. (See Figure 1–1.) The margins and vertical spacing you choose for your letter are important to its professional appearance. Your goal should be to place the message of your letter as close to the center of the page as possible. Short messages require lots of white space both horizontally and vertically, while long ones need to use up most of the space on the page.

HEADING

Most companies and organizations have their own printed letterheads, and consequently no return address needs to be typed in. On most letterheads the company name and address is centered on the page close to the top like this:

The American Heritage Bookstore
250 Central Avenue
Lyndon City, TX 75236

4-6 spaces

(letterhead   xxxxxxxxxxxxxxxxxx   (your name)

or   xxxxxxxxxxxxxx   (street)

heading)   xxxxxxxxxxxxxxxxxxxxxx (city, state, zip)

2-3 spaces

xxxxxxxxxxxxxxxxxxxxxxxxx   (dateline)

2-8 spaces

15 spaces

xxxxxxxxxxxxxxxxxxxxxxxx   (reader's name)
xxxxxxxxxxxxxxxxxxx   (title/department)
xxxxxxxxxxxxxxxxxxxxxxx   (company)   (inside   15 spaces
xxxxxxxxxxxxxxxx   (street)   address)
xxxxxxxxxxxxxxxx   (city, state, zip)

doublespace

Re: xxxxxxxxxxxxxxxxxxxxxxxxxxxxxxxxxxxxxxxxxx (subject line)

doublespace

Dear xxxxxxxxxxxxxxxxxxxxxxxx :   (salutation)

doublespace

xxxxxxxxxxxxxxxxxxxxxxxxxxxxxxxxxxxxxxxxxxxxxxxxxxxx
xxxxxxxxxxxxxxxxxxxxxxxxxxxxxxxxxxxxxxxxxxxxxxxxxx
xxxxxxxxxxxxxxxxxxxxxxxxxxxxxxxxxxxxxxxxxxxxxx.

doublespace

xxxxxxxxxxxxxxxxxxxxxxxxxxxxxxxxxxxxxxxxxxxxxxxxxx
xxxxxxxxxxxxxxxxxxxxxxxxxxxxxxxxxxxxxxxxxxxxxxxxxxx
xxxxxxxxxxxxxxxxxxxxxxxxxxxxxxxxxxxxxxxxxxxxxxxxxx
xxxxxxxxxxxxxxxxxxxxxxxxxxxxxxxxxxx.

doublespace

xxxxxxxxxxxxxxxxxxxxxxxxxxxxxxxxxxxxxxxxxxxxxxxxxxx
xxxxxxxxxxxxxxxxxxxxxxxxxxxxxxxxxxxxxxxxxxxxxxxxxx
xxxxxxxxxxxxxxxxxxxxxxxxxxxxxxxxxxxxxxxxxx.

doublespace

xxxxxxxxxxxxxxxxxxxxxxxxxxxxxxxxxxxxxxxxxxxxxxxxxxxx
xxxxxxxxxxxxxxxxxxxxxxxxxxxxxxxxxxxxxxxxxxx.

doublespace

xxxxxxxxxxxxxxx,   (complimentary close)

4 spaces

xxxxxxxxxxxxxxxxxxxxxxxxxx (your name)

doublespace

Encs.   (enclosure line)

doublespace

cc: xxxxxxxxxxxxxxxxxxxxx (copy notation)

4-6 spaces

FIGURE 1-1. An average-length letter in full-block style.

When you write letters about your personal business rather than your company business, type your name and home address at the top of the page. Don't use company letterhead for your personal correspondence. Of course, if you have the funds, you can order your own letterhead from a printer. Personal letterhead generally follows the same format as company letterhead, with your name and address centered at the top of the page. Personal stationery can be expensive, however. In addition, it is unnecessary. If you do not have personal stationery, it won't detract from the professionalism of your message. Just type your name and address four to six spaces from the top of a sheet of plain bond paper, centering each line and typing your name in capital letters:

ROBIN REDGRAVE

Lincoln Meadows, Apt. 4B
320 Sterling Street
Lyndon City, TX 75212

Although some established usage would put the writer's street and city address just above the dateline, and the writer's name only at the end of the letter, the method suggested here is better for two reasons:

1. It looks more like real stationery.
2. It enables readers to see at one glance, instead of two, all the information they need for the inside address of the return letter.

DATELINE

The date is typed two or three spaces below the heading flush with the left margin in the order of month, day, and year. Although the military and some formal organizations, such as law firms, sometimes type the day before the month, this is not standard American usage. Use cardinal numbers (1, 2, 3), not ordinal numbers (1st, 2nd, 3rd).

Right: September 12, 198_
Wrong: Sept. 12th, 198_
Wrong: 9-12-8_
Don't use: 12 September 198_

Do not abbreviate the month. As a general rule, you should avoid abbreviations in letter writing, except when they are parts of a legal name or title and where indicated in Appendix B as appropriate to letter format. For example, the abbreviations *Inc.* and *Co.* are commonly used in place of *Incorporated* and *Company* in an organization's legal name, and they should be written this way.

The data is important. If you leave it out and your letter is temporarily misplaced, the receiver may have difficulty interpreting and responding to your problem.

SPECIAL NOTATIONS

Instructions to the post office and/or the person who opens the envelope are typed next under the dateline. These notations include the following:

> Special Delivery
> Registered Mail*
> Certified Mail*
> Personal and Confidential

They are typed flush with the left margin, in capital letters, two spaces below the date. They serve as reminders to the typist to include the instruction on the envelope.

"PERSONAL AND CONFIDENTIAL" NOTATION

The words "Personal and Confidential" can be a useful signal to the reader when you want to ensure that only the addressee reads your letter. It is necessary only when you are writing to administrators who have their mail opened by someone else. Typed on the envelope, this notation acts as an attention-getting device, creating the impression that the letter is important and isolating it from the volume of everyday correspondence.

As a general rule, if it would prove embarrassing to you or the

---

*For a discussion of registered and certified mail, see p. 44.

person to whom your letter is addressed for an outside party to read it, type **Personal and Confidential** on the letter as well as on the envelope.*

This notation is not for everyday use. But if you want the business discussed in your letter to be kept confidential, or if you want to call attention to the urgency of your message, this is one way to do it. It can even form part of your total strategy. You can use it to reinforce the seriousness of a complaint about a product or service. Establishing this confidential tone at the outset makes your name and business stand out from the crowd.

The "Personal and Confidential" notation may be used with a letter of application for employment, particularly when you require that your candidacy not be revealed to anyone else—namely, your present employer.

Use this technique wisely and don't overdo it.

INSIDE ADDRESS

Skipping down two to eight spaces, depending on the length of your message, type the inside address flush with the left margin. The inside address includes:

1. The name of the person to whom the letter is addressed, including a courtesy title: Mr., M's, Dr., Professor, and the like.
2. His or her title and/or department.
3. Company name.
4. Street address.
5. City, state, zip code.

Here is an example:

Mr. Thomas Ireland
Vice President for Public Relations
Global Vision, Inc.
3200 Jefferson Blvd.
Reagansville, CA 92040

*See "The Envelope."

Courtesy Titles

It is always polite and businesslike, when addressing someone you've never met, to include a courtesy title in front of the name. Men, of course, are simply addressed as *Mr.* With women, however, you have a choice. Some women prefer being addressed as *Ms.* (pronounced *miz*), whether they are married or unmarried. On the other hand, some married women insist on *Mrs.*, while a few never-marrieds like to be called *Miss*. In our society's present state of flux over the Miss/Mrs./Ms. controversy you cannot always be sure how to address a woman without stepping on her toes.

For this reason, I recommend the use of *M's*, which neatly takes care of all three possibilities. *M's* can be read as:

1. A contraction representing *Miss*, with the *is* left out.
2. A shortened version of *Mrs.*, with the elimination of the *r*.
3. A variation of *Ms*.

Unless you know your reader's preference, the safe thing to do is to use *M's* for all correspondence addressed to women.

The only time you should not use *Mr.* or *M's* is when you don't know the sex of your reader. Perhaps you only know the initials of the company official to whom you are writing, or maybe you have before you one of those androgynous names like Leslie, Robin, Dana, Chris, Shelley, or Dale. Many men and women are offended when they are addressed as the opposite sex. So when in doubt about the sex of your reader, leave out the courtesy title in the inside address and salutation.*

If your addressee has earned a professional title such as *Dr.*, *Professor, Reverend, Senator,* or *General,* use that title instead of *Mr.* or *M's.*† These titles should appear before the name. In the case of medical doctors, dentists, and college professors, don't overdo your respect for the profession by affixing a degree after the name in addition to the courtesy title. One title is enough. For example:

Use: Dr. Naomi S. Feldman

  or

Naomi S. Feldman, M.D.
Not: Dr. Naomi S. Feldman, M.D.

*See "Salutation."

†See Appendix A for how to address government officials, clergy, and academic personnel.

Use: Dr. Harold El Nasser
       or
       Harold El Nasser, D.D.S.
Not: Dr. Harold El Nasser, D.D.S.

Use: Professor Harriet Hayes-Kennedy
       or
       Dr. Harriet Hayes-Kennedy
Not: Professor Harriet Hayes-Kennedy, Ph.D.
       or
       Dr. Harriet Hayes-Kennedy, Ph.D.

Esq., the abbreviation for *esquire*, a holdover from British custom, is the way American lawyers have traditionally addressed themselves. In some quarters it is no longer used, but legal practitioners, many of whom are still addicted to formality, may prefer it. If used, it should be typed after the lawyer's name, followed by *Attorney at Law* on the next line.

Example:
    Kenneth Blackhawke, Esq.
    Attorney at Law
    Marine Bank Building, Room 603
    Buffalo, NY 14205

Use it for both men and women. The wordsmiths have not yet developed a female equivalent for *esquire*.

Organizational Titles

Next should appear the job title of the person to whom you are writing. This is important, especially if the company or organization is large. Sometimes a quick telephone call to the company's switchboard will produce a title, or at least the name of the division or department in which the individual works.

It is best to place the organizational title or department name on the second line of the inside address, unless it and the reader's name are short. Set up the lines of the inside address so they are well balanced. Here is an example of an inside address that would be poorly balanced if the title were placed on the second line:

Balanced:

Mr. John H. Salerno, President
International Confederation of Publishers
8200 Douglass Parkway
Tanglewood, FL 32304

Not balanced:

Mr. John H. Salerno
President, International Confederation of Publishers
8200 Douglass Parkway
Tanglewood, FL 32304

Don't abbreviate the reader's title or department unless you need to produce an evenly distributed inside address. Some standard, acceptable abbreviations are listed in Appendix B.

You must have complete information in the inside address. Thorough attention to detail is very important, because what you type on the face of the letter will be repeated on the envelope. If the information on the envelope is incomplete or incorrect, your message may never reach the company; or it may reach the company, fall into the wrong hands, and get lost somewhere in the paper shuffle.

If your letter never reaches its destination or is delayed getting there, you will have wasted a lot of time and effort. For that reason, avoid sending your letter until you know the name and organizational position of the person in charge of taking care of your problem. Your local public library has reference books to help you with names, addresses, and phone numbers. Checking with the reference librarians before you send off your letter will pay dividends.

Company Name

Just as important is to remember to include the company name. Just think what would happen (and it does, every day) to a letter addressed this way:

M's Catherine Kopec
Assistant Vice President
2605 Avenue of the Americas
New York, NY 10022

You may be able to afford a mistake like this if the organization you aim to contact is located in a small town. Consider, however, how many companies share the facilities of a skyscraper on Sixth Avenue!

Street Address

Similarly, you might get by if you omit the street address for a large manufacturer based in a small town. In large cities, however, where any one organization is not highly visible, a letter without a street address is a dead letter.

City, State, and Zip Code

Finally, include the city, post office abbreviation for the state (refer to Table 1-1), and the zip code, which is readily available at your local post office. Don't second-guess the two-letter state abbreviations. Your letter may end up in Montana instead of Minnesota! Even if a correct zip code takes care of a misspelled state abbreviation, don't rely on the post office to set things right. You want your letter to reach its destination *quickly*.

ATTENTION LINE

Although you still see it in some commercial correspondence, attention lines are holdovers from the past. Years ago letters from one corporation to another were considered formal documents. Companies and firms did not address letters to individuals; they addressed them to corporations and then directed them to the attention of individuals within the corporate entity. The inside address, therefore, did not contain a person's name but merely the corporate name. An attention line was added to show where in the corporation the letter should be delivered, and the salutation was plural to reflect the total audience:

Global Vision, Inc.
3200 Jefferson Blvd.
Reagansville, CA 92040
Attn: Mr. Thomas Ireland
    Vice President for Public Relations

Gentlemen:

Today business correspondence is less formal and more personal. People reading business letters expect to be addressed by

TABLE 1–1. State abbreviations for use with zip codes.

Alabama	AL	Montana	MT
Alaska	AK	Nebraska	NE
Arizona	AZ	Nevada	NV
Arkansas	AR	New Hampshire	NH
California	CA	New Jersey	NJ
Canal Zone	CZ	New Mexico	NM
Colorado	CO	New York	NY
Connecticut	CT	North Carolina	NC
Delaware	DE	North Dakota	ND
District of Columbia	DC	Ohio	OH
Florida	FL	Oklahoma	OK
Georgia	GA	Oregon	OR
Guam	GU	Pennsylvania	PA
Hawaii	HI	Puerto Rico	PR
Idaho	ID	Rhode Island	RI
Illinois	IL	South Carolina	SC
Indiana	IN	South Dakota	SD
Iowa	IA	Tennessee	TN
Kansas	KS	Texas	TX
Kentucky	KY	Utah	UT
Louisiana	LA	Vermont	VT
Maine	ME	Virginia	VA
Maryland	MD	Virgin Islands	VI
Massachusetts	MA	Washington	WA
Michigan	MI	West Virginia	WV
Minnesota	MN	Wisconsin	WI
Mississippi	MS	Wyoming	WY
Missouri	MO		

name. *There is no longer a need for attention lines.* If you use them, you run into the dilemma of what to say in the salutation. *Dear Mr. Ireland* is not correct, because you haven't addressed the letter to Mr. Ireland. You have addressed it to Global Vision and must use a salutation that speaks to the whole company. *Gentlemen* is not appropriate, because a corporation's employees are no longer exclusively male. *Ladies and Gentlemen* strikes most readers as pompous and oratorical. For all these reasons, it is sensible to eliminate attention lines from business letters.

SUBJECT LINE

A subject line is a handy device for specifying what your letter is about before you begin. It aids the reader and anyone else who may have to handle your letter. Businesses process hundreds of letters a day. If you include a subject line you will help the company to sort and file its mail, as well as alert the reader to the content of your letter.

A subject line is not necessary if you haven't yet established a relationship with the company or if you are trying to create a personal atmosphere, as in a letter asking a favor. Do use one, however, if you have had previous business or correspondence with the company and can identify the subject briefly and concretely. A subject line should highlight exactly what the letter is about by referring to names, dates, times, places, numbers, and other quantitative data.

Although many business and government organizations use the word *Subject* to start off this line, the professions have traditionally used the abbreviation *Re*, a shortened form of *in re*, the Latin equivalent of *concerning*. *Re* is a crisp, legal term that adds a touch of class to a business letter. I recommend using it.

Double space after the inside address and type the subject line flush with the left margin. Then underline it so it stands out on the page. Here are some examples of well constructed subject lines:

Re: Your policy no. A698–586–2000

Re: London trip of October 14, 198_

Re: Property at 320 Sterling St., account no. 21102301000

Capitalize only the first word of the subject and all proper nouns.

Concise subject lines are useful and can add to the total professional appearance of your letter. But avoid using them if you can't sum up your business in a nutshell. Of no help to your readers is a subject line that is too general, like the following:

Re: Concerning your recent shipment

Concerning is redundant, since *Re* means just that. In addition, *your recent shipment* tells nothing about the shipment, not even its invoice or order number. The following, in contrast, cites the hard facts your reader needs to identify your problem quickly:

Re: Imperfect condition of TEN EASY STEPS TO
      DECORATING YOUR HOME, invoice no. 98600

Note that only the last line is underscored in a subject extending to two lines.

SALUTATION

Double space below the inside address or subject line, if you use one, and type the salutation flush with the left margin. In business letters, unlike personal letters, the salutation is followed by a colon, never a comma. A comma after the salutation in a business letter is gauche. Using it will make you appear an amateur in the eyes of your reader. So don't detract from the professional appearance of your letter by committing this common error.

I have stressed the importance of knowing the name of the individual who will handle your problem. When you know that name, constructing the salutation is simple. The salutation consists of the last name of the person to whom you are writing, preceded by a courtesy title and *Dear*:

Dear M's Kopec:

Dear Mr. Salerno:

Unless you know your readers on a first-name basis, it is neither businesslike nor politic to address them by their first names. Neither should you use the first *and* last name of your reader:

Bad form: Dear John:
Bad form: Dear Mr. John Salerno:

The only time you should include a first name in a salutation is when you don't know the sex of your reader or when you have only his or her initials. Then you must begin with:

Dear Chris McNulty:

or

Dear J. T. Moreau:

When your reader has a professional title, use it instead of *Mr.* or *M's*:

Dear Professor Tademaru:

Dear Reverend Carter:

Dear Senator Meerse:

Dear General Amiran:

If you have added a degree to the name of a dentist or medical doctor in the inside address, the salutation should read:

Dear Dr. Feldman:

The salutation for a lawyer, whether or not you have used the *Esq.* title, is:

Dear Mr. Blackhawke:

Although you should know your reader's name in most business situations, at times tracking down a person's name is neither possible nor feasible. When this happens and your inside address reveals only an organizational title, department, or company name, how do you construct the salutation?

Although ·ome companies have reacted to the problem by omitting the salutation entirely, most professionals today view a letter without a salutation unfavorably. Various changes have been made in business writing strategy over the past twenty-five years, and almost all of them reflect a more personal, conversational style. Eliminating the salutation is not in tune with this trend to personalize the business letter.

Dear Sir/Madam: is the best way out of that dilemma. It is the only practical choice in addressing an organization when you have no idea who your reader might be.

When you know the organizational title or division you want to reach, however, you may have an inside address that looks like this:

Manager
Grand Mal Hotel
500 Main Park West
New York, NY 10017

Dear Sir/Madam: is entirely appropriate in addressing this unknown manager, but so is *Dear Manager*. Here are some other salutations that work well:

Dear Director:

Dear Chairperson:

Dear Sales Representative:

Dear Dean:

Dear Coordinator:

When addressing an unknown manager, chairperson, or other organizational representative, choose the style you are most comfortable with. Either method will do. But when in doubt, use *Dear Sir/Madam*.

YOUR MESSAGE

After the salutation, double space and swing back to the left margin to begin your first paragraph. There is no need to indent paragraphs with the full-block format. Just remember to double space between each paragraph.

COMPLIMENTARY CLOSE

The last sentence of your message is followed by the complimentary close. Double space after your last paragraph and start it at the left margin. The following four closings are the most commonly used today:

> Sincerely yours,

> Sincerely,

> Cordially yours,

> Cordially,

Very truly yours, Yours truly, and variations thereof, though still used today, are more formal than they need to be. *Respectfully yours* belongs to the nineteenth century and should be avoided.* *Thank you* is never appropriate as a close. Your statement of appreciation should appear somewhere in the body of your letter.

When your closing comprises more than one word, capitalize only the first word. A comma always follows the close.

YOUR NAME AND ORGANIZATIONAL TITLE

Skip four spaces and type your name under the complimentary close at the left margin. You should not use a courtesy title with your name unless you have one of those androgynous names mentioned in the "Courtesy Titles" section. If you want your reader to know you are female or male, include a courtesy title before your name, but enclose it in parentheses and omit it from your signature:

> Sincerely yours,
>
> *Robin Redgrave*
>
> (M's) Robin Redgrave

*See first footnote of Appendix A.

When writing a letter on behalf of your organization or profession, it is not in good taste to include a professional degree (*J.D.*, *Ph.D.*, *Ed.D.*) after your name unless you are an *M.D.* or *D.D.S.* Nor should you prefix titles like *Professor*, *Dr.*, or *Senator* to your name. Do, however, include an organizational title or professional rank on the space immediately below your name, as in:

Harriet Hayes-Kennedy
Associate Professor of Psychology

Edward P. Meerse
United States Senator

Thomas Ireland
Vice President for Public Relations

Barbara Wardzinski
Sales Manager

Murray Klein
County Executive

Before sending off the letter, sign your name in the space between the complimentary close and your typed name. Use black or blue ink, never a pencil! Always remember to sign your name in this space. A letter loses its credibility when the author forgets to sign it.

REFERENCE INITIALS

If you have typed your own letter, no reference initials are needed at the bottom of the page. Sometimes, however, you may hand over your rough draft to a professional typist or dictate your letter to a stenographer. The person who types your letter will then include your initials (in capital letters) and hers or his (in lowercase letters) with a slash between them. These initials should appear two spaces below your typed name at the left margin, like this:

RR/jc

See Robin's letter to Horizon Publishing (Model No. 4).

These initials are generally of no interest to your readers, except perhaps to indicate that your status is high enough to support a secretary. Companies and organizations use them, nevertheless, for office documentation. File copies of correspondence are often reviewed after the originals have been mailed, and on some occasions it is useful to know who typed a letter. The dictator's initials are included because in some business situations a person other than the signer composes the letters.

ENCLOSURE LINE

The enclosure line is a signal to the reader that something is being enclosed with the letter. It is typed directly under the reference initials with no space in between. If no reference initials are used, type the enclosure line two spaces below your typed name.

Always use it when you are enclosing a check, order form, brochure, report, or other document with the letter. If you mention in the body of your letter what you have enclosed, type only the abbreviation *Enc.* or *Encs.* If more than one item accompanies the letter, show the number of items enclosed:

Encs. 3

If you don't mention somewhere in the letter that other papers accompany it, tell the reader here what items are included:

Encs. Contract
Check for $39.40

The enclosure line is important for two reasons. First, it signals to your readers immediately, before they read your letter, that you intended to include other papers. When they spot the enclosure line and see that no additional materials accompany the letter, they are alerted immediately to the omission. Those extra papers are often vital to a business transaction. It's important to document their presence.

Second, if you type the enclosure line at the bottom of your letter, you will remember to enclose the supporting documents when you mail it out.

COPY NOTATION

You may sometimes need to send a copy of your letter to other people concerned with your problem. (See Models No. 3 and No. 8.) When you send copies to other parties, show it by typing the copy notation. The copy notation lets your readers in on the fact that other people will receive a copy of your letter. This information may help them to judge the total situation and to decide on a course of action. It will also help you, as you are signing and folding up the letter, to remember to send out the copies.

Back in the days before photocopy machines were so popular, most companies used carbon paper to make extra copies of correspondence. Although many big organizations today use a Xerox or other copy machine to run off copies, a carbon copy is still cheaper to produce. If you are typing at home without access to a copier, use carbon and make your copies on onionskin. Simply type the lowercase letters *cc* followed by a colon, two spaces, and the name(s) of the person(s) to whom the copy is being sent. Position it a double space below the previous line of type.

cc: C. Vollaro
    N. S. Feldman, M.D.

No cover letter or explanation is needed when you send out the carbon copy. Place a checkmark (✓) in front of the individual's name, and sign your name in the signature space. Then fold the letter and place it in a properly addressed envelope.

If you choose to make a photocopy of your letter, use the letters *xc* instead of *cc*.

Perhaps you wish to send a copy of your letter to someone else and don't want your reader to know about it. Make what is known as *the blind carbon*. Since you don't want any notation to appear on the original, take the original letter and the first sheet of carbon paper out of the machine. Then type the following on the first and succeeding carbon copies, including your file copy:

bcc: C. Vollaro
     N. S. Feldman, M.D.

You have now indicated to the recipients of the copies and to yourself, but *not* to your reader, that copies have been sent to other interested parties.

POSTSCRIPT

Although the postscript is not often used in business letters, you *can* use it when you want to highlight an important point. In our personal letters, which are usually hastily put together, a P.S. is an afterthought—something we forgot to say in the body of the letter. In a carefully phrased and well executed business letter, however, a P.S. can act as a punchline.

Like the other special notations that appear outside the body of a letter, the *P.S.* attracts the attention of readers before they turn to the letter itself. Therefore, it should contain important information and, if possible, motivate your readers to read your letter carefully.

Imagine you are writing to the customer services division of a candy company about a nail you discovered in one of its candy bars. Outraged at losing a filling and part of a tooth, you explain every detail about the accident, which cost you $450 in the dentist's chair. Obviously the $450 bill is a vital part of your message. Instead of referring to it in the body of your letter, however, you could place it in a postscript:

> P.S. My dentist bill came to $450, for which I expect reimbursement.

The placement of this information outside the body of your letter accents its importance.

Here is another example of a carefully planned postscript:

> P.S. Effective August 1, 198__, my address will be:
> Lincoln Meadows, Apt. 4B, 320 Sterling Street,
> Lyndon City, TX 75212.

The placement of this important information in a postscript says to the reader—take notice!

You do not ever have to use a postscript in a business letter, but keep in mind that it can be effective if it ties in with the total strategy of your message.

Double space below the last notation on your letter and start the P.S. flush with the left margin. Then, after signing your name in the signature space, handwrite your initials below the last line, like this:

> P.S. My dentist bill came to $450, for which I
> expect reimbursement. *RR*

SECOND PAGE

Most business letters will fit onto one page if you follow the guidelines for spacing given earlier in this chapter. Sometimes, however, you may need to include a great deal of factual information or back-up detail to support an argument. In that case your letter will be longer than one page.

The second and succeeding pages of a letter are always typed on plain bond paper, not on letterhead. Don't put *your* name or address at the top. Starting four to six spaces from the top of the page, with the same margins you used on the first page, type at the left margin the name of the person you are addressing. Directly underneath type the date. On the third line type the page number. The three lines should be single spaced and look like this:

David L. Wong
September 13, 198—
Page 2

Then leave three lines of space and pick up where you left off on the preceding page.

THE ENVELOPE

When you have finished your letter, you are ready to type the envelope. Use a standard, legal size white envelope (No. 9 or 10). Unless your envelope has a printed return address, type your name and complete address in the upper left corner. Then skip to the center of the envelope, and, looking at your letter, type the inside address as it appears there, single-spacing the lines. That is all the information needed on the envelope, except for directions to the post office (such as *Special Delivery, Registered Mail,* or *Certified Mail*), and, if necessary, the special instructions *Personal and Confidential* to the person who will open it. These instructions should be typed a double space above and five spaces to the left of the reader's name and address. (See Figure 1–2.) A subject line is never typed on the envelope.

```
Robin Redgrave
Lincoln Meadows, Apt. 4B
320 Sterling Street                          (stamp)
Lyndon City, TX 75212


            SPECIAL DELIVERY

                 Mr. Thomas Ireland
                 Vice President for Public Relations
                 Global Vision, Inc.
                 3200 Jefferson Blvd.
                 Reagansville, CA 92040
```

FIGURE 1–2. Envelope format.

If you should for some reason use an attention line, type it to the left of the last line of the reader's address like this:

```
                          Global Vision, Inc.
                          3200 Jefferson Blvd.
                          Reagansville, CA 92040

Attn: Mr. Thomas Ireland
      Vice Pres. for Public Relations
```

Sign your letter if you haven't already done so, put enough postage on the envelope, mail it out, and wait for the results!

CHAPTER 2

MESSAGE

YOUR READERS, AS I explained in Chapter 1, will form their first impression of you from the way your letter *looks*. If your letter is neatly typed, with all parts in the right places, the reader is ready to develop some interest in what you have to say. This chapter will tell you how to organize your ideas to develop this interest and get your reader to see things your way.

Whenever you write a letter, you are either telling your readers something they need to know or asking them to do something for you. As a rule, you don't write business letters for any other reason. Thus all business letters involve problem solving, whether the problems are your own or your reader's.

Quite naturally, when you write you are most concerned with your own problems. If you need to make a hotel reservation in a distant city, to obtain information about a company's product, to get a refund for damaged merchandise, or to look for a new job, you send out a letter because you wish to make changes in your life. You want these changes to be effected smoothly.

At first glance your reader may appear to have no interest in your affairs. Communication, however, is always a two-way street. You may *think* you are all alone with your problem. If you stop to think about it, however, you'll realize the person on the other end has problems too and that they're related to yours. Your reader and you have something in common, or you would not be writing the letter. It is this common *something*, this basis for empathy, that you need to discover and make use of.

If a letter cannot result in appropriate action it should probably not be written. A business letter is always judged first by the usefulness of its information. If you don't have anything useful to say to your reader, don't write the letter. The price of paper products has escalated dramatically during the last ten years. So has the cost of secretarial help, postage, and office supplies. The Dartnell Target Survey estimates that, as of 1984, it costs $8.10 for businesses to dictate, transcribe, and send out a letter.* Is this letter you're thinking of writing designed to achieve results or will it waste your time, money, and energy? If the latter is the case, rethink your objectives.

Suppose you *do* have a clear objective in mind. If so, before writing your letter, stop to think whether there might be a better method of communicating the information. Often a telephone call is a cheaper and quicker way to take care of your business. Remember, though, that phone calls are shortlived. When you conduct your business by telephone, you place your trust in the good memory of the person on the other end. The written word, on the other hand, is less likely to be forgotten or misplaced. In deciding between telephoning and writing, consider well your time limits and the urgency of your message.

Sometimes personal contact has more effect than a letter. Suppose you are seeking funds for a charity or civic group. You will need to determine, based on the time and expense involved, whether you should write a letter or solicit an individual in person. Asking people for money is always a precarious business, requiring much tact and interpersonal skill. Consider carefully whether a face-to-face contact might make a better first impression. Often it does, but don't forget that your meeting will have to be followed up by something in writing.

In addition to fundraising problems, many confidential matters are handled best in a face-to-face or telephone conversation. Personal criticism or touchy subject matter, where a person's reputation or career (including your own) might be at stake, may be better communicated by a phone call or visit, especially if you're not totally confident of your way with words or want to feel someone out before

*This dollar amount was researched and published by The Dartnell Corporation (4660 Ravenswood Avenue, Chicago, Illinois), which has been releasing this information since 1930.

getting to your point. Perhaps you are sending a message that may be unwelcome to your reader, and you are unable to soften the blow through the written word. Be fair to the reader and yourself. If you feel you can handle the problem best through personal contact, then do so.

When you have finally decided the problem should be approached through a letter, focus on two things as you plan your message—purpose and audience.

PURPOSE

Make sure you never lose sight of the purpose of your letter. Many people, including those who should know better, think that business letters are vehicles for showing off their knowledge. Others use the letter as a vent for letting off steam. A business communication, however, should never be used for one-upmanship or acrimonious assaults on the reader. Remember, you're writing the letter because you have a job to do. You won't achieve the desired results if you focus on establishing your superiority over the reader.

The principal purpose of all business communication is to tell readers what they need to know to solve your problem. By giving information, you may also help your readers solve their own problems by guiding them into action or persuading them to accept a point of view. Keep in mind at all times that your problem is also a problem to your reader; if you do that, you will stay on base.

Letters are written to evoke reactions from the reader that will lead to a resolution of or a change in your affairs. In that sense, most business letters are sales letters, whether a product, service, or idea is being sold. When you write a letter you are trying to convince someone to act or react in a positive way. If you were writing a short story or poem, you might wish to use abstract words or metaphors to express your ideas. Abstractions and metaphors, however, leave themselves open to different interpretations. When writing for businesspeople, therefore, stick to a plain style and concrete words. Your reader will be able to respond quickly to your problem only if your meaning is absolutely clear.

AUDIENCE

The reason we don't use figurative and fancy language in a business letter has to do with our consideration for our audience. Fiction writers and poets write to an undefined audience of people who are free to choose whether they wish to read their works. Businesspeople, on the other hand, have no such choice in their reading material. They are expected to read incoming mail, and for this reason—because they *must* read it—you need to be careful about *what* you say and *how* you say it.

The audience of a business letter differs from that of a short story or poem in yet another respect. In most cases people who write business letters address one person. They have to visualize that person and what that person wants and needs to hear. Because fiction writers communicate feelings and thoughts to the general public, they don't visualize their audience in the same way. A business writer addresses a specific, carefully defined audience and must keep that audience constantly in mind.

The fact that you have no personal knowledge of your reader should not hinder you from analyzing your audience. You do not need to know the personality or character of your readers to write success-ful business letters. All you have to do is speculate on their business needs, which are based on their occupations and positions within an organization. Throughout the planning of your letter think about what *the reader* wants to know, what *you* want him to know, and what *reactions* you want from him. The better you can visualize your read-er's situation, the better chance you stand of getting that person to see things your way. Furthermore—and this is *very* important—assume, unless you know otherwise, that your reader is intelligent but unin-formed. Don't talk down to the reader. Instead, convey your respect.

THE RIGHT BEGINNING

In keeping with that respect, be aware that your readers are busy people who have a lot of mail to read and answer. Management people are in a hurry; they must read their mail quickly and are turned off if they have to wade through a lot of material to get to the main point. Therefore, the most important part of any business com-munication is the beginning.

If your readers are not attracted to the very first paragraph, they may fail to see the importance of your letter and toss it aside for later reading, thereby delaying a response. Or they may proceed to read it for the wrong things. The beginning affects the readability of the entire letter.

There are two ways to open a business letter—directly or indirectly. The first, or direct, style is more common. It is used in three of the basic letter types discussed in this book—the Letter of Request, Letter of Complaint, and Letter of Application. The indirect style is illustrated in the Letter of Refusal and Letter of Persuasion.

Use the Direct Style for Most Letters

Although you may be able to get away with leading up to the main point in a very short letter, in most correspondence the purpose of the letter should be stated in the first paragraph. Even if you have identified your problem in a subject line, always start out by telling the reader why you are writing the letter. In other words, begin with the most important point you need to get across.

Do this by either asking a question or making a statement. Then follow your request or statement with your reasons for making the request or with supporting detail for your statement.

Lead into a Negative or Unexpected Message

Considerably more caution should be adopted when you are writing a letter of refusal or persuasion. Because your message may not be welcomed or expected, postpone the main point until you have established empathy with your reader. Only after you have prepared your reader can you communicate the bad news or the request firmly and confidently.

Whichever style you use, make sure that first paragraph attracts the reader's attention.*

TONE

With proper attention to purpose and audience, you will arrive at a good beginning for your letter—one that will spark your reader's interest and encourage a favorable reaction. To sustain that interest, however, you must be conscious of the tone of voice you convey.

Be Positive

Adopt an attitude of mind that is positive, secure, and free from doubt. Your reader will be judging you and your problem according

---

*The next five chapters elaborate on the direct and indirect styles.

to the strength of your position, and your position will be weak if you sound like someone who has no command over your own destiny. Perhaps you *are* unsure about the issue at stake or what can or should be done about it. Nevertheless, don't transmit this uncertainty to your reader. Never suggest that you're still trying to make up your mind about what you expect from the reader. You should have formed your expectations before you began to write. If you reflect uncertainty, your letter will affect the reader unfavorably and lessen your credibility.

Take a stand. Right or wrong, you very often have only one chance to state your case. A letter that wavers and falters over an issue usually is not taken seriously. Opt for a positive tone, one that clearly indicates you know what you are about.

Show that *you* understand your problem and express confidence that your reader will understand it. Don't complain, apologize, beg, or plead. Always remember you are writing about a business transaction and can expect your readers to be interested in serving your business needs *and* their own.

To avoid a negative impression, guard against phrasing that suggests the reader will not agree with you or take the action you request. Be especially watchful for *if clauses* that imply your reader has two ways to look at the problem. Here are some examples:

Negative:
If you think my claim for tax abatement is justified, please send me a check.

Positive:
I will appreciate your check for $108 in settlement of this claim.

Negative:
If you think I qualify for the position of office manager, please call me for an interview.

Positive:
I look forward to talking with you about my qualifications for the office manager position.

Avoid weak words like *hope, may, might, perhaps,* and *maybe* when they imply the reader may not do what you expect.

Examples:
Negative:
Because you have been active in our community's recycling project, I thought you *might* wish to join our Energy Conservation Committee.
Positive:
Since you have been active in our community's recycling project, I am sure you will want to join our Energy Conservation Committee.

Negative:
Perhaps I should inform the Better Business Bureau about the kind of operation you're running.
Positive:
I intend to inform the Better Business Bureau about the problem I have had with your product.

Negative:
I *hope* you will be able to send me some information about Global Vision's semi-rigid, gas-permeable lenses.
Positive:
Will you please send me some information about Global Vision's semi-rigid, gas-permeable lenses?

A positive tone is especially important in nonroutine correspondence in which you ask your reader to make an extra effort to accommodate you. For example, you may have to turn down an invitation to collaborate on a project. Or you may request funding for a cause important to you but not necessarily to your reader. Another letter requiring special care is a request for adjustment on a bill when there is disagreement about who's at fault. In these complex situations you must create a confident atmosphere to persuade your reader that your position is justified.

In developing a positive tone, take care not to present false information or deceive the reader. Neither should you cover up any important details related to your problem. Deliver the facts with the strength of your convictions about them, and you will more likely than not convince your reader that your point of view is legitimate.

Adopt the Reader's Point of View

A self-assured, positive tone depends on your assessment of your reader's needs. Sometimes these needs are tangible ones directly related to the reader's desire to perform effectively for an organization. At other times you may want to satisfy intangible needs, such as your reader's desire for personal or social recognition. Always try to anticipate how your problem will affect your readers and devise a strategy that will take into account their problems as well as yours. Your assessment of your reader's needs is especially important when you deliver disappointing news or try to persuade an unwilling stranger to accept your ideas.

All letters, however, require a determined effort on the part of the writer to adopt a *you attitude*. That means you must interpret the facts in terms of what they may mean to your reader, as well as what they mean to you or your company. Advertising people are skillful in conveying a *you attitude*; when they try to get you to buy a product they always tell you how much you need it. Although you don't want your letters to sound like promotional hypes, develop some insight into your readers' motivations and let them know you're aware of *their* needs and responsibilities.

Put yourself in the reader's place. What would you need to know if you were in that person's shoes? What would you like to hear? How do you want to be treated? If you can achieve a proper balance of the reader's needs with yours, your chances of reaching a solution to your problem improve.

Although this method does not lend itself to easy prescriptions, one way to express concern for your reader is to make liberal use of the words *you* and *your*. Whenever you can, turn your sentences around by using *you* instead of *I* or *we* to let your readers know you have their interests in mind:

> *Not:* *We* would like you to contribute to our Energy Conservation Campaign.
> *Rather:* *You* are one of the people who can make our Energy Conservation Campaign a success.

> *Not:* *I* have six years' experience managing a large city bookstore.
> *Rather:* Six years of experience running a large city bookstore will help me to manage *your* purchasing department effectively.

Even routine business letters will be improved by emphasizing the reader rather than the writer:

I attitude: I received your letter of February 8.
You attitude: Thank *you* for your letter of February 8.
We attitude: *Our* new contact lens will be advertised in the <u>New York Times</u> next week.
You attitude: *You'll* read about our new contact lens in the <u>New York Times</u> next week.

Simple, matter-of-fact information can often be rephrased to create empathy:

Cold: *Our* company policy does not allow *us* to make payment unless *we* have a copy of the bill.
Warm: Because our company is committed to protecting *you*, the customer, *you* will understand why we need a copy of the bill before we can pay *you*.

Cold: The merchandise you shipped on July 2 was defective.
Warm: *You* can imagine my disappointment when I discovered the merchandise you shipped on July 2 was defective.

Cold: *We* cannot accept this merchandise.
Warm: *You* can understand, I am sure, why this merchandise is not acceptable.

In general, you will help your case by judiciously using the pronoun *you* to filter attitudes of good will through your letters.

In some business situations, however, a warm, friendly *you attitude* is neither desirable nor feasible. (See Model No. 3 in Chapter 4.) You may need to establish your authority by adopting a strong, demanding tone. Even so, retain a conscious sense of your reader's responsibilities. A *you attitude* may be only implicit in what you say. It will still be effective.

LENGTH

Many people, unfamiliar with the business world and instilled with the time-honored notions of brevity and clarity, falsely assume that all business letters should be short. Brevity, to be sure, is a characteristic of all good writing and worthy of respect. However, brevity in *words*, not *ideas*, is the ultimate goal. All business communications should say everything that needs to be said in as few words as possible. That means *don't leave out any important ideas*.

Although most business letters seldom run longer than two pages, the length of your letter depends on how much information your readers need to enable them to work on your problem. Constant evaluation of your purpose and audience will determine how much your readers need to know. Make sure you give them the right amount of information—neither too much nor too little. While you don't want to present your reader with an isolated fact irrelevant to the problem, neither should you omit details that may help him or her solve it.

Economy of words is an important requisite to a good business letter. Just don't confuse it with economy of ideas. In other words, be generous with your facts.

Like Robin Redgrave, who writes the letters in this book, you will often need to write to solve a problem. The five general types discussed here—letter of request, letter of complaint, letter of refusal, letter of persuasion, and letter of application—cover most writing situations. Study their strategies. When your message does not lend itself to one of these general classifications, reconstruct the models to develop a strategy that fits your special purpose.

The models described in the following five chapters will provide you with the basic elements of business letter strategy, whether you write as a consumer or as a representative of a business or nonprofit organization. Follow them whenever you write to a business, a customer, a government official, or a fellow citizen.

CHAPTER 3

THE LETTER OF REQUEST

WHEN YOU ASK for information, goods, or services from an organization that is in business to supply its products or services, you generally expect that it will react favorably to your request. This is why a letter of request is the simplest to write.

USE THE DIRECT APPROACH

Whether you're writing to a company that has advertised through the media or to an organization you may have heard of by word of mouth, you can rest assured the reader will be willing to comply with your request if you include all the information needed to act upon it. Therefore don't delay stating the purpose of your letter. The direct style is always best for a routine letter of request.

Most people feel they should explain the steps leading up to their decision to write before they make the request. Although background information is generally useful to your reader, it should not be placed at the beginning. Get to the point right away so your reader can see immediately what is expected. Whether you're writing to a manufacturer to order a product, to a hotel to make a reservation, or to a company for an employment reference, state the purpose of your letter first; provide background and explanations later.

In Model No. 1, Robin makes her request to Global Vision in the form of a question. This question is followed by her reasons for asking it. She then asks a series of specific questions relating to the general one. This question technique draws attention to Robin's problem immediately.

If you use the question approach, you may choose to begin your letter with one of the specific questions, perhaps the fifth one in the series. If Robin had opened her letter with *Is there a distributor of Global Vision's lenses in southern Texas?* she might have stimulated even more interest in her problem. Specific and precise, this question commands attention. On a hot, drowsy day such an energetic approach might motivate Thomas Ireland to respond more quickly to Robin's problem.

It doesn't matter greatly, however, which type of question you use—the general or specific. Just remember that the more interesting the beginning is, the more receptive your audience will be to reading further and acting on your problem.

Of course, you don't have to open with a question. Perhaps a simple statement is more appropriate to your purpose:

I would like to order 25 gallons of Pilgrim Interior Latex Paint as advertised on page 5 of your spring catalog.

or

Please cancel my membership in the Executive Book Club.

Whether a question or statement, your opener should contain the purpose of your letter.

EXPLAIN YOUR PROBLEM

Once you have cleared the air by stating your goal, you are ready to tell your reader where you heard about the product or service, how much you already know about it, and why you are interested in finding out more. This middle section of your letter should contain all the facts the reader needs to respond to your request.

Because businesses are usually interested in knowing the results of their advertising, you should tell them where or how you learned of their services. Robin's letter acknowledges that FORTUNE magazine is the source of her inquiry.

ROBIN REDGRAVE
Lincoln Meadows, Apt. 4B
320 Sterling Street
Lyndon City, TX 75212

November 15, 198_

Mr. Thomas Ireland
Vice President for Public Relations
Global Vision, Inc.
3200 Jefferson Blvd.
Reagansville, CA 92040

Dear Mr. Ireland:

Will you please send me some information about Global Vision's
semi-rigid, gas-permeable lenses?

In a recent Fortune article (October 10, 198_) on new contact
lens technology, I read that your company has developed and
marketed this new lens. I have been wearing hard contacts for
ten years but want to switch to a softer, more comfortable lens.
Because I have astigmatism, however, the traditional soft lens
doesn't fit my needs. Your new lens, according to the Fortune
article, can be shaped to correct for astigmatism.

I will be thankful for any information you can send. In addition,
I would like answers to the following questions:

1. Can they be worn during the night; i.e., are they designed
   for extended wear?

2. What has been the success rate for wearers so far?

3. What is the price to the consumer?

4. Has a bifocal been designed for this type of lens?

5. Where are the lenses being distributed? Is there a
   distributor in my area?

Since my optometrist is uninformed about your new lens, I will
greatly appreciate your help.

Sincerely yours,

Robin Redgrave

(M's) Robin Redgrave

MODEL NO. 1. Letter of request.

In addition, the more you explain your problem and how it relates to the company's services, the better prepared the reader will be to follow through with the right information. Robin's request to Ireland is complex. Because she wants concrete, special facts about the new contact lens (facts that might not be contained in a single pamphlet), she outlines some specific details of her vision problem, leading into the five questions she poses in the next paragraph. By explaining her problem in detail, she justifies her request and increases her chances of getting a complete answer.

EXPRESS APPRECIATION

Your letter of request should close with an expression of appreciation carefully coordinated with the subject of the letter. Avoid platitudes, such as *Thank you in advance for your assistance in this matter* or *I will appreciate hearing from you at your earliest convenience.* (See Chapter 8 for a complete discussion of rubber stamps that are inappropriate in today's business world.)

Tailor your statement of appreciation to an idea that ties it to the principal message. The fact that Robin's optometrist does not carry the new Global Vision lens provides Ireland with a new thought related to her purpose in writing the letter. This thought should spur him on to broaden his company's share of the contact lens industry.

Robin's letter to Global Vision relies on her assessment of Ireland's commitment to his company and its public service goals. Not all letters of request, however, need this studied an approach. A simple order letter, for example, requires little more than a paragraph or two setting forth complete information about the product requested (catalog number, size, color, amount, price, and so on), the method of payment, the source of the writer's information about the company, and perhaps a deadline for delivery. Expressions of gratitude can often be omitted in such routine order letters.

Another problem needing limited explanation is a request for a hotel room. Robin's work as a bookstore manager requires her to attend many business conventions. In her letter to the Grand Mal Hotel (Model No. 2), she reserves her room well in advance of the convention to ensure an exciting view of the New York landscape.

ROBIN REDGRAVE
Lincoln Meadows, Apt. 4B
320 Sterling Street
Lyndon City, TX 75212

November 22, 198_

Manager
Grand Mal Hotel
500 Main Park West
New York, NY 10017

Dear Sir/Madam:

Please reserve a double room for me and my husband
for the nights of January 6 and 7.

We will be arriving in New York on the morning of
January 6 to attend a convention of the National
Booksellers Association, which has recommended
your hotel. We would appreciate a room on one of
the top floors overlooking the park, to be charged
to my VISA Account No. 0999 280 672 894.

Please confirm in writing that you're holding the
room.

Sincerely,

Robin Redgrave

(M's) Robin Redgrave

MODEL NO. 2. Letter of request.

Because no negative reaction is generally expected, the letter of request is the simplest form of business letter to write. The complaint letter, discussed next, demands more careful attention to strategy and tone.

CHAPTER 4

THE LETTER OF COMPLAINT

PROBABLY NOTHING IN our busy lives is more exasperating than the consumer ripoff. Defective coffeemakers, service station bungles, landlord or tenant difficulties—all test our patience and challenge our ability to carry on everyday routines. Sometimes these problems are relatively minor and cause only temporary inconvenience. Yet remembering Ford's problems with the Pinto, we should be aware that corporate irresponsibility can, and does, endanger lives. Manufacturers can try to conceal poor quality control methods, but when an issue erupts in a lawsuit or reaches the press, they're liable for damages or bad publicity. When you pick up your local newspaper to read reports of nails, glass, and other foreign objects found in candy bars and cereals, or of decomposed rats residing in pop bottles, it should be evident that your consumer problems are also big business's problems.

You, as well as the corporation or public service agency, have the right and responsibility to protect yourself. Why suffer in silence when a well constructed letter of complaint may result in the return of your investment and the relief of your conscience?

It stands to reason that corporations and service organizations wish to retain the good will of the consumer. That's why they're in business. In the course of ordinary business these organizations receive many letters from dissatisfied consumers about unfair treatment or defective products. Some of them end up in the circular file, others remain for months in the unfinished business pile, and some are acted on immediately. You want to ensure that *your* letter will be one of those receiving a quick response. Follow these simple guidelines for success.

KEEP COOL

A clear head works wonders. Let the initial shock, disappointment, or anger wear off before you think about the letter. Many complaint letters fail because the writer is not in a problem-solving mood. So give yourself a couple of days to cool off before you sit down at the typewriter.

WRITE TO THE RIGHT PERSON

Complaint letters often fail because they are addressed to someone deep within the corporate or government bureaucracy who lacks the initiative or power to resolve the problem. Customer service departments are, it is true, designed to handle consumer complaints and might therefore seem a reasonable route to the settlement of your claim. Remember, however, that customer service departments in large corporations receive hundreds of claim letters every day, and they get behind in answering their mail. The president of the corporation gets fewer letters.

Send your letter to the most powerful person in the organization. The principals of large organizations, often removed from the day-to-day operation of the business, may be more interested than some of their employees in what customers or constituents are thinking. If they are not and have instructed their secretaries to refer all complaints to the appropriate department, there is one thing you can do to get your letter to their desks. Use the *Personal and Confidential* strategy discussed in Chapter 1. Many secretaries are instructed not to open an envelope marked in this way.

Perhaps the president or chief officer will read your letter, decide not to deal with it, and refer it to someone else for a response. If this occurs, it will be to your advantage to have your letter delivered to the responder from the president's office. Knowing their bosses are aware of a complaint often provides employees with an incentive to handle the problem swiftly.

In addition, writing to the chief officer simplifies the task of determining the right person to whom to deliver your complaint, for you can feel confident he or she will send it to the right department.

As an example, consider Robin's dilemma over her school tax in Model No. 3. Having moved to Texas from New York State, she was unfamiliar with Lyndon City's method of levying property taxes. When she bought her condominium she wrote a check to the bank to cover her school tax when it came due. During the turmoil of the move and her new job managing the American Heritage Bookstore, she assumed the tax collection agency would forward the bill to the bank for payment. Naturally she was upset when several months later she received a bill that included a finance charge for late payment.

Upon querying Oil City Savings and Loan, she was told that her problem was common among new home buyers. The tax bill, instead of going directly to the bank, is sent to the property owner by the city. Unfortunately the mechanism for recording the property transfer at the County Office Building is slow, sometimes taking several months. Consequently the tax bill in question must have been forwarded to the previous owners, who neglected to send it to Robin.

Understandably, Robin feels the charge is unfair. She is not in the habit of paying bills she never receives. Moreover, she is doubly annoyed because $1200 of her money has been sitting in the bank for six months without collecting interest. Protesting to the bank vice president, she is told there is nothing the bank can do; the problem is between her and Lyndon City. Having warned her that most residents have little success with the city's tax department, Mr. Vollaro at Oil City Savings offers to mark her bill *Paid under Protest*, advising her to pay the full amount to avoid further interest charges.

Instead of scuffling with City Hall, Robin sends her letter to Murray Klein, the elected official in charge of administering the policies and regulations of the county. Since she anticipates a difference of opinion about who is at fault, she predicts that the person who oversees the local agencies is the most likely prospect for settling her claim.

SHOW THEM YOU MEAN BUSINESS

Robin knows she faces a difficult problem, about which she doesn't know the legal rules. Furthermore, she realizes a lawyer would probably charge her more than the $76 she is after. But she does have the

ROBIN REDGRAVE
Lincoln Meadows, Apt. 4B
320 Sterling Street
Lyndon City, TX 75212

February 2, 198_

CERTIFIED MAIL

Mr. Murray Klein
County Executive
County Office Building
Lyndon City, TX 75230

Re: Property at 320 Sterling St., account no. 21102301000

Dear Mr. Klein:

Oil City Savings and Loan Association has suggested I write you about a charge for late payment of school taxes incorrectly applied to my account. On January 20, under protest, I paid a bill for $1,218.37 to the Receiver of Taxes in Lyndon City, $75.87 of which represents a fine for late payment. This charge is unfair.

When I bought the Sterling Street condominium on July 31, 198_ I was unacquainted with Lyndon City, its method of levying taxes, and the tax due dates, having been a resident of New York State for 16 years. At the closing I turned over to Oil City Savings and Loan, the bank holding my mortgage, $1,142.50 for payment of the school tax when it came due. I was unaware the City would not be sending the tax bill directly to Oil City Savings.

Because I never received a bill for the school tax, which I am told was issued late in September, I was surprised when, in January, I received a bill for $1,142.50 plus the late payment fine of $75.87. I understand now, after talking with the City tax collectors, that they sent the September bill to Mr. and Mrs. Richard Graf, the former owners of the property, who neglected to forward it to me.

Enclosed is a copy of the bill I paid under protest. I intend to contact the Consumer Protection Bureau of Texas within two weeks if the sum of $75.87 is not reimbursed me.

Therefore I will appreciate your looking into the problem, Mr. Klein, and asking the proper agency to return that amount to me.

Sincerely,

Robin Redgrave

(M's) Robin Redgrave

Enc.

cc: C. Vollaro, Oil City Savings

MODEL NO. 3. Letter of complaint.

43

clear conviction that her rights as a citizen have been violated, and she intends to put that idea across firmly. She states positively, therefore, in the first paragraph, that the charge was incorrectly added to her account, and later that she has been unfairly treated. Moreover, she informs Klein she will appeal to a state agency if she receives no satisfaction from him, giving him two weeks in which to respond.

The letter is sent *certified mail*, another indication the writer means business. A certified letter requesting a return receipt presents proof that your letter has been received, for a mail carrier will not deliver it until a receipt has been signed at the other end. The receipt is then returned to you. When you want to ensure that your reader receives your message, it is worth the extra investment to send your letter certified mail.*

Note that nothing in Robin's letter incites the reader to take offense. Subdued in tone, her letter appeals to Klein in a matter-of-fact style designed to attract his attention and respect. All facts relating to the problem are included—account number, property address, full dollar amounts, pertinent dates, name of the bank, and a copy of the bill in question. No facts have been omitted, and Oil City Savings is properly notified of her action with a carbon copy. The hard facts she outlines lend credibility to her claim. So does the order in which she presents them. This is how to arrange your ideas in a complaint letter.

SUMMARIZE THE PROBLEM AND YOUR POSITION

Robin uses the direct approach. Her opening paragraph presents a capsule description of the problem and her purpose in writing the letter. Adding strength to her claim, she explains that the Oil City bank has encouraged her to protest the charge. The first paragraph, therefore, introduces the problem in a way that discourages the reader from questioning her claim.

PRESENT THE BACKGROUND DETAILS

After identifying the problem, Robin provides a chronological account of the events leading to it. The following two paragraphs attempt to

*The slightly more expensive *registered* letter serves the same function, the difference being that registered mail can be *insured*. Whenever you send a valuable item through the mail, ship it *registered mail*, return receipt requested. The postal employee will record its value, which you will receive if the item is lost or stolen. See page 6.

justify her claim with evidence. Beginning with a cogent appeal explaining her vulnerable status as a new resident of Lyndon City, she ends the second paragraph stating she was not sufficiently informed to avert the problem that later arose.

The undercurrent running through the next paragraph appeals to the common sense of the reader. Essentially, the question is *Who pays bills that are never received?* Without accusing anyone directly, she lays the burden on the tax collector and the former owners of the property—on the former for sending the bill to the wrong party, on the latter for not forwarding it to her. Robin seeks to make it clear *she* was not at fault.

ASK FOR AN ADJUSTMENT

After exhausting the facts at her disposal, Robin turns the letter around to the tough stance adopted in the opening paragraph. Inviting Klein to examine the bill, she matter-of-factly states she will report the problem to the Consumer Protection Bureau if her bill is not adjusted. To ensure that her claim will be evaluated promptly, she sets a time limit of two weeks for Klein to respond.

The final paragraph softens the hard line taken in paragraph four by expressing appreciation for what she confidently expects Klein will do. Furthermore, in referring to Klein by name, she creates an atmosphere of good will and empathy.

Mild or implied threats often serve a useful purpose in letters of complaint. A call or trip to your public library will produce the names and addresses of local and national consumer groups, the Better Business Bureau, and regulatory agencies such as the FDA, ICC, FTC, and EPA. The mere mention of one of these agencies can inspire the reader to listen to you, as can a subtle reference to your lawyer. Some people believe showing on the face of the letter that a carbon copy was sent to a regulatory agency or lawyer will result in quicker action. To determine how strong a position you need to take, consider the severity of the problem and judge your reader well.

Robin Redgrave's letter to Murray Klein demanded a great deal of thought, for, as in so many consumer problems, the situation is not cut and dried. Robin's case may not hold up in court and she knows it. Therefore, she needs to act as her own lawyer to convince her reader her claim is justified.

Not all problems, however, require so concentrated a strategy.

The American Heritage Bookstore
250 Central Avenue
Lyndon City, TX 75236

ROBIN REDGRAVE, Manager   (814) 973-1000

December 5, 198_

M's Barbara Wardzinski
Sales Manager
Horizon Publishing Company
82 Salinas Street
Little Apple, WI 53405

Re: Imperfect condition of TEN EASY STEPS TO DECORATING
     YOUR HOME, invoice no. 98600

Dear M's Wardzinski:

Our order of 100 copies of Ten Easy Steps to Decorating
Your Home by Lenore Goodman, order no. RC28, which
arrived yesterday from your warehouse, is not suitable
for sale.

We were eagerly awaiting the arrival of this publication
after its favorable review in Publishers Weekly. In fact,
several of our regular customers have already requested
the book. You can imagine our disappointment, therefore,
when we opened the shipment to find a large faded spot
across the upper lefthand corner of each of the covers.

Since the book should prove to be a popular gift item,
you can understand why we cannot accept this shipment.
We are therefore returning the cartons to your warehouse
today and asking that you send a duplicate order right
away.

Since we need these books for our Christmas sales, we are
confident you'll get the duplicate order to us quickly.

Sincerely,

Robin Redgrave

(M's) Robin Redgrave
Manager

RR/jc

MODEL NO. 4. Letter of Complaint

46

Damaged products, incorrect shipments, and pricing errors, for example, are problems that will need less planning on your part.

When you don't expect your reader to question your claim, the most important ingredient of a complaint letter is a clear recital of the facts. Robin's letter to the Horizon Publishing Company (Model No. 4) is an example of such a routine claim.

Identifying the problem in a subject line, Robin summarizes the purpose of her letter in the first paragraph and then moves on to specific details in the second. In complimenting the company on the marketability of the book, she establishes good will, motivating Wardzinski to correct the problem quickly. Then, pointing out that she herself has acted quickly in returning the books, she tells the company exactly what to do to straighten out the order. Finally, the closing statement expresses confidence that Horizon will act immediately.

The letter covers all the facts needed for Horizon to check on the shipment in its files: American Heritage's order number, their own invoice number, the title and author of the book, the number of copies sent, and the date the books were received at the American Heritage Bookstore.

A direct approach, a cool, firm tone of voice, plenty of hard facts, and a specific demand will result in a letter of complaint that stands a good chance of achieving its goal. Always remember your goal and singlemindedly strive toward it. If you digress in anger or accusation, your reader will lose faith in your argument, and *you* may lose your case.

So far, singlemindedness of purpose has pointed the way to successful letters of request and complaint. Let's look now at a problem that requires a double vision.

CHAPTER **5**

THE LETTER OF REFUSAL

WHEN YOUR BUSINESS calls for refusing a request or delivering bad news, you will find that analyzing your letter's purpose is more difficult. On the surface your only goal may seem to be to respond to the request. Yet when your message carries bad news, you also need to anticipate the reactions of your reader. The two letter types discussed thus far (the letter of request and letter of complaint) focus on the resolution of *your* problems. In a letter of refusal, however, you are responding to someone else's problems and must give your reader's interests priority over yours.

When you have unwelcome information for your reader, your objective becomes double-edged: Not only must you transmit the bad news, you must also keep the reader favorably disposed to you. Your message is destined to create a problem for your reader, since one anticipates good news and is seldom prepared for the bad. Therefore, when you inform your readers they have exceeded their credit limits, have failed to make timely payments, or have been unsuccessful in landing a job, put yourself in their place to determine how best to soften the blow. When you must refuse an order or cancel an account, you always stand the chance of losing the reader's good will. Keep in mind your twofold purpose—to convey the unpleasant information *and* to retain the reader's good will—and you will succeed in sustaining a good business relationship.

This total concern for your reader calls for an indirect approach.

Unlike the letter of request or complaint, the letter of refusal will not benefit from beginning with your most important point, namely, the statement of refusal. Those who fail to appreciate this principle and who start off a letter with *I regret to inform you that* . . . show no regard for the person at the other end. Set up your readers by delivering the news gracefully. Prepare them by creating an atmosphere in which they can feel good about themselves and their relationship with you. Only after your reader is in a good frame of mind should you disclose the hard facts.

OPEN WITH A
POSITIVE STATEMENT TO ESTABLISH EMPATHY

Almost any time you must deny the reader's request you can find something for which to communicate your thanks or concern. Perhaps you have had a satisfactory business relationship with your reader in the past. Here is an opportunity to express appreciation for that business.

If the reader is soliciting you for employment, show appreciation for the interest expressed in your company. If you are asked to attend a meeting as a guest speaker, begin by showing your respondent that you are flattered by the invitation. Even unfavorable responses to complaint letters can establish empathy through concern for the reader's dilemma. In your first paragraph express a genuine interest in your reader without suggesting your position on the problem. Only one side of your dual purpose should be revealed here—that of retaining your reader's good will.

DISCLOSE THE BACKGROUND INFORMATION

Follow up your expression of good will by explaining the reasons leading to your decision to refuse the request. Include all relevant facts so the reader can't fail to perceive *your* dilemma. If your refusal seems arbitrary you will diminish or destroy the empathy created in your opening paragraph.

This section of your letter should be well developed. If you sufficiently support your position, you can shift emphasis away from the refusal by momentarily allowing your readers to see your problems instead of their own.

Guard against saying more than you have to, however. Overlong explanations may make readers impatient or give the impression you are softsoaping them. Without beating around the bush, give them all the evidence they need to understand *your* problem.

STATE THE REFUSAL

Your denial of the request should be the logical outcome of your explanations leading to it, and it should not be longer than one sentence. If you have thoroughly outlined the reasons for your decision, saying no will be easier. By this time the reader will be receptive to your second objective—conveying the bad news itself. Don't dwell on this negative portion of your message. State it quickly and concisely.

PRESENT ALTERNATIVES OR OFFER SUGGESTIONS

If you can think of other ways in which your readers can solve their problems, develop some positive alternatives. The strategy behind a letter of refusal is to make the bad news seem less important than it is. Therefore, any suggestions you can offer will deemphasize the negative content and encourage gratitude on the part of your reader. For example, if you must turn down a speaking engagement, perhaps you can propose a substitute speaker. A request for an out-of-stock item can often be remedied by another product. Alternatives judiciously offered will accentuate the good will you seek to convey.

If no alternatives are possible, build on empathy by developing a positive outlook on the reader's situation. If you must refuse a customer credit, explain the benefits of buying on a cash basis. When you turn down job applicants, perhaps you can assure them that their qualifications are strong and their opportunities for employment elsewhere promising.

These additional thoughts may not always be necessary or possible. When you offer them, however, you increase your chances of sustaining a healthy business relationship with your reader.

CLOSE ON A FRIENDLY NOTE

Continue the positive tone you have built up in the foregoing paragraphs with a brief but friendly close. If you want your readers to respond, tell them how to do it.

AVOID NEGATIVE WORDS

Your letter of refusal will be easy to compose if you employ the behavioral psychologist's tactic of being positive. Simply approach the negative situation with a positive attitude, and you will allay your readers' disappointment and convince them you mean well.

This positive perspective is enhanced when you avoid negative words. Since all your efforts have been devoted to presenting your message in its most positive light, be sure to choose your words carefully so that no disagreeable connotations creep in. When we have to deny a request, the first words that come to mind are words like *sorry, cannot, regret,* and *inconvenience*. With careful revision we can eliminate these psychologically unpleasant reminders of the refusal.

Stress what you *have* done, *can* do, or *will* do instead of what you haven't, can't, or won't do by avoiding words like *no, not, cannot,* and *will not*. In addition, the words *refuse, turn down, reject, regret, unfortunately, misunderstanding,* and *mistake* counteract the empathy you are striving for. While you might want to use these words in a complaint letter, in a letter of refusal minimize the disagreeable aspects of the situation by avoiding them.

Words with negative implications remind your readers that their interests are threatened. So do profuse expressions of apology. Statements like *I'm sorry* or *please accept my apologies*, while not negative in themselves, weaken your reasons for refusal. If you have fully explained your reasons, there is no need to apologize for them. Excessive apologies build up psychological resistance to the message and can neutralize your good will effort. After all, you have made a sound, legitimate decision. Why apologize?

Robin Redgrave's problem with a publisher's faulty printing was the subject of Model No. 4. When she realized, however, that Horizon was not going to send a new order in time for the holidays, her problem was compounded. Her customers, like Mrs. Washington in Model No. 5, planned to use these books as Christmas presents. Knowing Mrs. Washington was anxiously awaiting the arrival of Ten Easy Steps to Decorating Your Home, Robin designed her letter tactfully.

Her letter represents an affirmative approach to Donna Washington's problem. All details pertaining to the order—author, title, number, and price—are included in a subject line to remind the customer of her original request. Robin then establishes empathy in

The American Heritage Bookstore
250 Central Avenue
Lyndon City, TX 75236

ROBIN REDGRAVE, Manager   (814) 973-1000

December 13, 198_

Mrs. Donna Washington
28 Franklin Road
Pelham, TX 75215

Re: Your order for 12 copies of Lenore Goodman, TEN EASY
     STEPS TO DECORATING YOUR HOME ($14.95)

Dear Mrs. Washington:

Your order for the above book, placed last month when you
were in our store, is, as always, greatly appreciated.
We are anxious to please faithful customers like you by
satisfying all your requests with quality merchandise.

Horizon Publishing Company, the distributor of this
excellent book, has recently experienced operational
difficulties at its plant. When your copies arrived
here from Horizon's Wisconsin warehouse on December 4,
we discovered a noticeable flaw in the color pattern of
the front cover. Knowing you need these books for
Christmas presents, we immediately reshipped them to
Horizon's warehouse and requested a duplicate order.

Just today, Barbara Wardzinski, Horizon's sales manager,
telephoned to explain that her press is working overtime
to reprint the covers. The new shipment will reach us on
December 27. We are therefore unable to have these books
for you before Christmas, as we had originally promised.

Although arriving too late for a December 25 delivery, Mrs.
Washington, the books will be here in time for delivery by
January 1. We therefore suggest you send us the names and
addresses on your gift list, along with your personal
holiday message on the gift cards enclosed with this letter.
We will giftwrap the 12 books on December 27 and send them
out special delivery. Your friends will receive them no
later than January 1.

If this arrangement is not satisfactory, two other books
popular during this holiday season may suggest a suitable
alternative. Berle Johnson's Four Seasons Gourmet Cookbook
($10.95) and Walter Hampton's The Making of a City: Lyndon
City's Architectural Origins ($15.98) both make excellent

MODEL NO. 5. Letter of refusal.

Mrs. Washington
December 13, 198_
Page 2

gifts. If you telephone me collect before December 20,
the day of our truck deliveries to Pelham, you will
receive these books that day.

Please let us know how we should handle your order.
We want you to enjoy the best holiday season ever.

Cordially,

Robin

Robin Redgrave
Manager

RR/jc

Encs.: 12 gift cards with envelopes

the opening paragraph by showing appreciation and willingness to provide good service. American Heritage's desire to furnish quality merchandise, which closes the paragraph, leads into the explanation that follows. It is precisely because the store insists on quality for its customers that Mrs. Washington's order is being delayed.

The reason American Heritage can't deliver on time is explained in the next two paragraphs. Complimenting the customer on her wise choice, with reference to this *excellent* book, Robin summarizes the problem by citing names, places, and dates. This thorough attention to detail assures Mrs. Washington her problem is in good hands and that all parties to the order are working together.

By the time the letter arrives at its secondary purpose—transmitting the bad news—Mrs. Washington is prepared to receive the message that her Christmas presents won't be ready on December 25. The refusal is stated clearly. Yet because it is sandwiched into the middle of the letter at the *end* of a paragraph, it is minimized.

Although the opening clause of the fourth paragraph relates to the bad news already revealed, the use of Mrs. Washington's name personalizes the message, reminding the customer that her concerns are top priority in this letter.

Robin then addresses the alternatives available to Mrs. Washington. By enclosing gift cards and offering to deliver the books by the New Year, she makes the first alternative as convenient as possible. She then meets Mrs. Washington's objections to this proposal by suggesting two similar gift items of comparable price, either of which can be delivered before Christmas.

In the closing paragraph Robin asks the customer for instructions and expresses her desire to make Mrs. Washington's Christmas a merry one. By signing only her first name, she sustains the familiar, personal tone of her letter.

The positive approach of Robin's letter is supported by her affirmative language. The letter consistently emphasizes what American Heritage *has* done, *can* do, and *will* do to satisfy the customer's needs. Because she avoids using the overworked word *unfortunately*, Robin's statement of refusal subtly diminishes the disagreeable nature of the situation. Nowhere in the letter does she *regret the inconvenience* suffered by the customer or *apologize* for it. Every effort is made to assuage Mrs. Washington's disappointment on receiving the letter.

Because the implicit purpose of this letter was to encourage a

The American Heritage Bookstore
250 Central Avenue
Lyndon City, TX 75236

ROBIN REDGRAVE, Manager   (814) 973-1000

April 17, 198_

Mr. Juan Perez
69 Roosevelt Parkway
Lyndon City, TX 75230

Dear Mr. Perez:

Thank you for your response to our recent advertisement in the Lyndon City Courier Express for an
assistant manager. We sincerely appreciate your
interest in working for the American Heritage Bookstore.

Your many years of experience in retail sales would be
an asset to our bookstore. The assistant manager's
position, however, also requires a background in
accounting. Because several applicants for the position
have strong qualifications in accounting as well as
customer service, we are choosing the assistant manager
from among them.

Your excellent background in sales will undoubtedly
enable you to find a job more closely fitting your
qualifications. We wish you well in your job search.

Cordially,

Robin Redgrave

(M's) Robin Redgrave

RR/jc

MODEL NO. 6. Letter of refusal.

regular customer to continue a longstanding business relationship, Mrs. Washington's problem required a careful appraisal of her needs and an analysis of alternative ways to satisfy them.

Less effort is needed when you refuse requests from people with whom you are unacquainted or with whom you may not expect to do business. Such an example is Model No. 6 written to an individual looking for employment with the American Heritage Bookstore.

Robin's letter to Juan Perez works on creating empathy in the opening and closing paragraphs and reserving the bad news for a backseat position in the middle paragraph. The predominance of *you* and *your* over *we* and *our*, especially in the final paragraph, contributes to the letter's concern for its reader. *Your many years of experience* and *Your excellent background in sales* are examples of how to stress the reader's interests instead of your own (see pages 30–32).

Robin can offer no alternative to Juan's situation. However, her attitude to his employment prospects elsewhere is optimistic, and her kind closing remarks guarantee Juan will hold American Heritage management in high regard in the future. As in her letter to Donna Washington, Robin succeeds in maintaining a favorable image of her business.

Non-profit volunteer organizations also need to sustain good public relations. We will next see Robin engaged on behalf of the Lyndon City community, as she tackles the letter of persuasion.

CHAPTER **6**

THE LETTER OF PERSUASION

OUTFITTED WITH BRAND new contact lenses, Robin is now comfortably settled in her modern condo and has hired an assistant dedicated to helping her run the bookstore. She is finding time to take part in community activities. As a newly appointed organizer of an urban rehabilitation project, she now faces the task of designing a letter to a select group of Lyndon City residents, persuading them to help restore a National Historic Landmark.

A COMMUNITY-BASED PROJECT

Robin's experience with promotional literature as a bookseller has prepared her for this most difficult of all letter-writing assignments—the letter of persuasion. Yet most of us, untrained in the art of rhetoric, can use some tips in composing a letter motivating citizens to contribute to a cause. Longer than the average business letter, the letter of persuasion demands imagination and much planning.

When you try to convince someone to join a cause, buy a product, or subscribe to a service, the first thing you must do is analyze your audience. In a persuasive letter this analysis requires an examination of your readers' biological, emotional, and rational needs. Not surprisingly, selling an idea is often more difficult than selling a product or service. To move someone to accept your ideas, you sometimes have to create a whole new state of mind in your audience, a state of mind that will stimulate readers to satisfy those needs you have discovered and presented to them.

Work Up Some Enthusiasm for Your Project

To create a receptive attitude in another person requires that you yourself show enthusiasm for your ideas. Many sales letters fail because their writers lack genuine enthusiasm for what they are selling. Enthusiasm, like the flu, is infectious. You really have to be a little bit of a fanatic to inspire others to adopt your beliefs.

Therefore, in planning your letter, work first on reviving your own interest in the project. Examine your problem closely. Work backwards. What are you asking your readers to do? Why should they want to do it? In what possible ways will complying with your request benefit your readers? In exploring these questions you automatically bring your own interests, prejudices, and opinions to the surface and identify them with your reader's. That is how it should be.

Only by speculating on your reader's likes, dislikes, values, and fears—through examining *your own*—do you begin to fully appreciate the importance of the project you are promoting. The point is that you become more committed when you investigate the motives behind your commitment. Sometimes these motives are self-evident. Most of the time, however, they have been laid aside or forgotten in the hustle and bustle of more routine business. Before you can sway others to accept your ideas, you need to analyze your motives and assume your reader will share them.

Of course, your audience may not always share your likes, dislikes, values, and fears. This is a risk you take. Yet in working for the betterment of a community or organization you have an obligation to it. Your goal in writing the letter was decided on when you were assigned the task. You have a job to do. You *need* to take chances.

Discover and Create Some Reader Motives

An analysis of the motives behind your commitment to the project provides the basis for the whole strategy of your letter. Your readers must be persuaded they have good reasons to do as you wish them to.

What are some of the motives to which you can appeal? We are all creatures of necessity. Although some of our biological needs (such as food, drink, and clothing) are of the greatest urgency in our lives, our emotional, social, and intellectual pursuits provide the means to long-term security. It is usually these emotional, social, and intellectual requirements of life that readers identify with most readily.

Here are some of the motives to which a persuasive message can appeal:

- The satisfaction of appetite (hunger, thirst, sex)
- The need to have a roof over one's head
- The desire for clean, sanitary living conditions
- The desire for good health
- The need to protect family and loved ones
- The desire for safety and comfort—both physical and financial
- The profit motive (making and saving money)
- The desire to protect personal, community, and national reputations
- The desire for love and popularity
- The satisfaction of curiosity
- The need for humor and escape from boredom
- The desire for beauty and style
- The longing for knowledge and wisdom
- The humanitarian instinct to be generous and help others
- The need to maintain moral standards
- The satisfaction of retaining one's individuality
- Pride (in anything)
- The desire for success and prestige
- The desire to avoid criticism

Refer to this list when planning the strategy of a persuasive letter. Your appeal can be based on a single motive, but more often than not you can offer your reader a variety of reasons to join your cause or buy your product.

Once you have discovered some motives around which you can work your message, carefully develop, elaborate, and feed them. Organizing a sane, sensible appeal by cultivating reader motivation is a long, painstaking process. For you must lead your reader from one motive to the next, blending one with another and backtracking occasionally to reinforce earlier motives, all the while employing a *you attitude* and endowing the whole with a positive tone.

Once you have thought through the motives on which you will base your appeal, you can begin to structure your letter. A letter of persuasion is composed of three main parts—the three A's:

1. Attract *attention*.
2. Build an *argument*.
3. Ask for *action*.

Attract Attention

In most persuasive writing situations you're addressing someone who hasn't invited the letter. Usually this person is a stranger to you and, like most people, suspicious of new ideas, especially those that threaten to lighten the pocketbook. You should therefore not use the direct approach. Instead, first capture the reader's attention by stimulating some interest in your subject. Delay stating the purpose of your letter until you build up this interest, establish credibility, and state your case.

Get the reader involved. There is no simple prescription for attracting your reader's attention in a persuasive letter. Making an educated guess about what will whet your reader's curiosity calls for imagination, empathy, and, above all, a clear understanding of your reader's possible motives. The best opener is the one that gets the reader personally involved in your message.

Tact, subtlety, and a soft sell are needed to get your readers involved. Telling a human interest story or chatting about experiences you have in common are often effective ways to get them in the mood to receive your message. Since your goal in this first phase is to arouse mental activity and curiosity, a question will often attract attention. If you use the question technique, however, make sure the mental activity you stir up relates to the subject of your letter. Otherwise, your reader will distrust your honesty *and* your intelligence.

The opening paragraphs of Robin's City Hall preservation letter (Model No. 7) are questions that capture the reader's attention. Leading up to the milestone year of 1897, Robin recalls the excitement of the World's Fair, the inauguration of a president, and the opening of a

CITY HALL PRESERVATION COMMITTEE

HEADQUARTERS
1257 Truman Boulevard
Lyndon City, TX 75234

September 13, 198_

Mr. David L. Wong
12 Douglass Parkway
Lyndon City, TX 75210

Dear Mr. Wong:

Do you remember the festive atmosphere of Lyndon City in 1972 when we hosted the World's Fair out at Lincoln Meadows?

Can you recall the excitement in 1964, the year our native son, Lyndon B. Johnson, was elected President of these United States?

Were you here in 1942 when Lyndon City State University opened its doors to us?

Although most of us were not around in 1897, that too was a landmark year in the history of our city. For it was in 1897 that the old City Hall, designed by Louis Sullivan, changed the future of American architecture.

You probably know that Sullivan's building, the first tall, metal-framed structure in the United States, is internationally known as one of his finest early skyscrapers.

Eighty-five years ago Sullivan's steel frame and vertical lines contrasted with the classic Greek and Roman styles of his contemporaries. Today, his building stands apart from the severe, stark exteriors of our modern highrise office buildings.

When did you last stand on the corner of Webster and Court Streets to marvel at the magnificent floral designs and geometric ornament etched in the ruddy terra cotta surface of the building?

In his new book about Lyndon City Walter Hampton writes about "the subtle and studied relationship of ornament to structure" of this architectural treasure. Apart from ornament, the Sullivan building's bold, uplifting vertical lines represented, in 1897, the new direction of American architecture.

There are many 19th-century buildings left standing in the United States today, but except for the Burbane Building in Chicago, old

MODEL NO. 7. Letter of persuasion.

David L. Wong
September 13, 198_
Page 2

City Hall is the only example of the early skyscraper still alive.
It has been proclaimed one of the ten most important buildings in
the United States because it represents a truly <u>American</u> architecture.

Of course age alone does not determine a landmark's value. The
White House and Mount Vernon, for example, are older buildings
that impress us with a sense of history. Next to our own Sullivan
building, however, they are not architectural masterpieces. Why?
Because they are copies of European buildings, which were themselves copies of classical structures.

<u>We</u> have something <u>unique</u> in our city.

What has happened to old City Hall since 1897?

Sullivan's gift was the seat of our local government until 1957,
when Lyndon City ran out of funds to modernize the interior and
construct a more efficient airconditioning system. When the new
City Hall opened for business, the Sullivan building was converted
to a commercial office building and leased to a number of small
businesses.

It survived in this way until 1977, when a small fire in one of
the offices frightened city officials into closing it to occupancy. Since then the city has been looking for a developer who
will restore this masterwork as faithfully as possible to its
original character and convert it into a high-quality office
building.

Hard times are upon us, however. An out-of-state investment group
has offered to buy the property for $200,000. This group plans to
tear it down and build an apartment complex on the site.

The loss of the Sullivan building will deprive Lyndon City of a
major part of its heritage. As one of the bright stars of our
city, it has been attracting tourists for years and will attract
more in years to come. It is a structure we can truly be proud of.

Your pride in Lyndon City and its cultural traditions can help
save this historical landmark.

MODEL NO. 7. (cont.)

David L. Wong
September 13, 198_
Page 3

Recently Time magazine reported that 60 percent of the historical
landmarks present in 1955 are gone today. The cities and countryside are losing their traditions and the educational value that
resides in them. Our national landmarks help us understand our
history.

Your support is needed to preserve our great American cultural
heritage.

Many architectural historians are standing by to see if Lyndon
City has the courage to fight for its most famous architectural
landmark.

One individual in particular is watching us. Sidney Larson, a
retired architect and historian from St. Louis, is so interested
in our building that he would like to organize an Architectural
Museum and Information Center right here in Lyndon City within
the walls of old City Hall.

Mr. Larson has expressed interest in moving here to coordinate the
activities of the new museum, which would be the first architectural
museum in the United States.

Our City Hall Preservation Committee is trying to raise $1.1 million--
$200,000 to buy the building from the city and $900,000 to convert
it to modern office space.

We need to raise the money by January 1 to prevent Changeling
Investors, a Chicago firm, from destroying one of the world's most
celebrated office buildings.

As a result of negotiations with Mayor Brogan, the federal Economic
Development Administration has promised to provide us with $100,000
towards the rehabilitation of our landmark.

Mayor Brogan has personally pledged $2,000 to the preservation
campaign.

Sidney Larson has sent his check for $1,000.

Each of us on the Preservation Committee has pledged $1,000.

We have $123,000 toward our goal. Now we need civic and business
leaders like you to come forward and assist in this great undertaking.

David L. Wong
September 13, 198_
Page 4

Won't you join the mayor, Sidney Larson, and all of us on the
committee to ensure that Sullivan's building will grace our city
for years to come?

Let's all pull together to maintain our community's reputation.

Please contribute what you can to help save this endangered landmark. You can place your check, made out to the City Hall Preservation Committee, in the self-addressed, stamped envelope enclosed.

Maybe "you can't fight City Hall," as they say. But the time has
come to fight for it! Please join the fight.

Sincerely,

Robin Redgrave

Robin Redgrave, Chairperson

RR/mk

Enc.

MODEL NO. 7. (cont.)

university before zeroing in on a less well-known event—the design and construction of a famous building. By leading gradually into the subject of her letter—Sullivan's old City Hall—she arouses curiosity at the same time she sets up the strategy of her appeal.

Establish a common bond between you and your reader. This strategy centers around her development of motive. Each of her questions, emphasized by isolation in a separate paragraph, appeals to the reader's nostalgia for the past. By naming some important years in Lyndon City's history, Robin arouses interest at the same time she establishes a bond between reader and writer. As residents, both reader and writer are intimately connected with Lyndon City's past.

Using the personal pronoun *you* as well as the collective *we*, her thought-provoking questions immediately draw the reader into the images she creates:

- *Do you remember . . . when we . . .*
- *Can you recall . . . our native son . . .*
- *Were you here . . . when Lyndon City State University opened its doors to us?*

Singling out readers with the empathetic *you*, she identifies with them in her use of *we*, *our*, and *us*, creating a rapport at the outset.

Nostalgia for local history is the dominant motive to which Robin appeals in the first four paragraphs. Implicit within that appeal is a secondary, underlying motive—pride in Lyndon city. That secondary motive, implied but never stated in the opening paragraphs, later becomes, through the careful development of her argument, the central appeal of the letter. As we will see, she does not focus immediately on this central motive. She develops it slowly.

Having thus aroused her reader's interest, Robin begins thinking about the second phase of her letter.

How much do her readers know about old City Hall? They may know a lot; they may know little. Since the letter will be mass-mailed to hundreds, perhaps thousands, of city residents, she cannot judge the prior knowledge of her readers. As she considers how best to sustain the reader's interest, she decides that, to appeal to all possible readers, it's better to say more than less.

Build an Argument

Having attracted your reader's attention, you now try to keep it by providing some background and explanation for your opening. This middle section, or *argument*, is the longest section of the letter, for now you must justify fully the request you will later make.

Your reader's needs and motives are of paramount importance in building your argument. Yet so are the motives of the cause you're promoting. For readers may understand the personal benefits, tangible and intangible, to be derived from contributing to a cause. However, if they are not convinced that the project itself is worth the trouble or expense, or that it *needs* help, your letter will not succeed.

Therefore, how well you justify your request depends also on how well you interpret the needs of your project. Robin has to show, first, that the Sullivan building is worthy of preservation and, second, that its existence is endangered. She therefore organizes her argument around these two ideas, steering the reader toward the final section of the letter, the action section.

Describe fully the ideas behind your cause.   Give evidence that what you are "selling" is important. Every persuasive letter, whether it attempts to talk the reader into buying a product, an idea, or a recommendation, must describe its subject well. Readers expect to be fully informed when they buy. Because they will have no opportunity to question you verbally, you need to anticipate all possible questions and answer them.

Obviously, the kind of evidence you put forth is related to how you have evaluated your reader's motives. The two work hand in hand. You want to deliver the evidence that will satisfy your readers.

The vivid, thorough description of the Sullivan building in the fifth paragraph provides evidence, first, that the building is important enough to be saved and, second, that it cannot be saved without the reader's support.

This detailed description of the building reinforces the appeals to nostalgia and pride in the opening of the letter by introducing still other motivating factors. In explaining its distinctive character as the first skyscraper in the United States, Robin portrays the Sullivan building as a prime example of truly American architecture. She convinces us of its claim to distinction by concentrating on specific features of the building. From observing that the building is special, her readers infer that Lyndon City, its home, is a special place. Finally, the readers, as part of the city, conclude that they share in this distinction.

This is a quiet form of flattery—understated, implicit, subtle. Persuasive letters demand this gentle massage of the reader's ego. Unfortunately, too many of the sales pitches sent through the mail today carry the flattery principle too far, insulting the readers' intelligence and causing them to doubt the writer's sincerity.

The reader's satisfaction in harboring an architectural masterpiece is the motive being created. It is supported by examples of other, more famous buildings that have less claim to distinction. Thus, Robin exposes one piece of evidence that the Sullivan building should be saved.

Still another motive is revealed in the rhetorical question posed in the seventh paragraph—*When did you last stand on the corner of Webster and Court Streets . . . ?* Evoking an emotional response, this question directs attention to the beauty of the monument and offers still another reason for the reader to be proud of the building.

By concretely describing the building—its materials, its style, its claim to fame—Robin proves its merit at the same time she brings to light motives for the reader to respond favorably: the desire for distinction . . . the appreciation of beauty. A feeling of pride, the central motive appealed to, is being constructed through a steady accumulation of supporting motives.

Climaxing her detailed description of the building in the attention-getting one-liner—*We have something unique in our city*—Robin turns to the second rationale for her project. Having shown the Sullivan building is *worth* preserving, she will now show why it *needs* help.

Slowly reveal the purpose of the letter. Effective letters of persuasion lead gradually into the main idea (in this case, to ask for funds to preserve an historical landmark). If readers are told the purpose of the letter near the beginning, before their interest in your cause has been aroused, they may not be encouraged to read on, and you may have lost your chance to win them over.

Only when Robin is well into her argument does the reader discover why the condition of the Sullivan building is so thoroughly described. When readers learn what has happened to the old City Hall since 1977, they are finally alerted to the building's need for funds if it is to remain a city landmark.

In outlining the recent deterioration of the building and the danger of its demolition, Robin suggests more benefits to be gained if the building can be preserved: The city will protect its reputation, continue to attract tourists, preserve a means of educating citizens about American architecture, and retain its prestige as a cultural center. All these benefits to the city, which can be translated into benefits to the reader, strengthen the central motive of pride in one's community.

Having developed, but not stated, this central motive in the preceding paragraphs, Robin precisely defines it at the bottom of page two: *Your pride in Lyndon City and its cultural traditions can help save this historical landmark.* This subjective, you-oriented statement points to the reader's direct responsibility for the preservation project.

After guiding her readers through two pages of Lyndon City history, Robin has now singled each reader out as one whose cooperation is needed for the landmark's survival. How can she influence the reader to cooperate?

Provide testimonials.   Readers of persuasive letters often need assurance that others are supporting the cause before they feel committed to joining it. If your readers know that other public-spirited citizens have committed themselves, they will feel more inclined to comply with your request. The more testimonials you can provide, the more believable your project becomes.

Community volunteers who aren't themselves experts in a subject often solicit professional opinion to bolster their persuasive appeals. Reference to the opinions of experts can strengthen a persuasive letter.

Earlier in the letter Robin quoted from Walter Hampton's book on Lyndon City architecture to dramatize the unique character of the Sullivan building. As a further testimonial, she now introduces another authority—Sidney Larson, retired architect and historian. Explaining Larson's interest in the building, Robin creates another motivating factor for her reader. If the building is preserved, Larson plans to establish another "first" for the city—a museum devoted to American architecture.

Filling her letter with solid facts, Robin provides more testimonials by naming the individuals and agencies that have already pledged financial support. By obtaining federal funds and digging into his own pocket, the mayor has firmly illustrated his commitment. So has Sidney Larson, together with every member of the Preservation Committee, the writer included. By citing professional opinion and support, Robin shows the project is already underway. The reader is thereby assured there is precedent for joining the cause.

In addition to who is supporting your cause, your readers want to know the financial factors of the project. Robin has stated how much funding is required, how much has been pledged, and when the money is needed, providing as much financial detail as she can.

Use knowledge to build feelings. The preceding strategy depends on a logical ordering of facts, facts that are based on the writer's knowledge of her subject and her judgment of the reader's values. In slowly releasing these facts, Robin expects her reader to accept the reasonableness of her argument. But she expects her reader to respond to it emotionally as well.

In selling products or services, you can often appeal directly to a reader's immediate, material needs—increased profits, greater operating efficiency, or individual comfort. Yet in selling an idea, which is what Robin is doing when she asks for donations to the City Hall preservation project, you need to focus on readers' sense of values— their desire for social recognition, humanitarian instincts, or pride in their accomplishments.

Both jobs require a consistent, rational presentation of facts. Yet persuading people they will gain intangible benefits by joining a cause depends also on how well you stimulate an emotional response in them. How can you manipulate your facts to build up an emotional atmosphere?

One example of this process at work can be seen in the first three paragraphs on page 3 of the letter. The first sentence, reporting a statistic from *Time*, states that 60 percent of the landmarks in existence in 1955 are missing today. From this quantitative data Robin makes a deductive leap: Our educational resources are fast disappearing, for historic landmarks serve to teach citizens about great events of the past. The *Time* magazine statistic has little emotional color. The conclusion she derives from it, on the other hand, invites an emotional response.

In the one-sentence paragraph that follows, Robin intensifies the emotional atmosphere by pleading for the reader's support. Then, by reporting that historians are *standing by to see if Lyndon City has the courage to fight*, she gently challenges readers to summon up their own courage. The vivid words *standing by*, *the courage to fight*, and *watching us* create a mental picture that increases the emotional charge.

That emotional charge is grounded on one small statistic from the pages of *Time* magazine. This is but one example of how to use your knowledge to create emotional responses in your reader.

Throughout the argument section of her letter, Robin has been quietly nourishing her readers' sense of importance by setting in front of them various motives for joining the cause. Reinforced by testimonials from expert witnesses and a steady sprinkling of *you* and *your*, these motives are by now firmly embedded in readers' minds. It is time to push for a response.

Ask for Action

If you have worked hard at justifying your cause by anticipating all possible reader motives, the final, action phase of your letter will proceed smoothly. In the preceding paragraphs you have hinted at the action you wish your reader to take. Now you must make a direct request.

Be specific by telling your readers exactly what to do. Whenever possible, make it easy for them to respond by enclosing reply forms and self-addressed envelopes.

Don't come on too strong or too weak. A too aggressive approach, implying the reader has no right to refuse your request, will destroy the good will you have been so carefully nurturing. On the other hand, maintain a confident attitude by avoiding weak words and phrases that suggest the reader may not take the action you expect. (See pages 28–30.)

In explaining what your readers must do to comply with your request, remind them of the advantages to be gained. Picking up on one of her earlier themes, Robin reminds her readers that their sponsorship of the Sullivan building will protect the future reputation of the city.

Stay clear of cliches in your closing remarks. (See pages 37 and 144–146.) *Thank you in advance for your cooperation* and *Please do not hesitate to call on me if you have any questions* have no place in this or any other business letter. They are stale and trite. Your readers shouldn't have any questions if you've done your homework. If they take your argument seriously and still have questions, you can be sure they will contact you without a special invitation to do so.

End your letter as appealingly as you began it. Try a play on words, as Robin does. Or simply stop with your request for funds.

Keep the Typography Simple

Since many of my readers may be planning campaigns similar to Robin's, I would like to pass along a word or two of advice about mass-produced letters.

Most readers, especially those favored by membership on scores of mailing lists, tend to regard anything that looks like a sales letter as junk mail. Consequently, thousands of persuasive letters are discarded soon after their delivery to the mail box. Sometimes the envelope is never opened.

Large organizations that solicit subscriptions and contributions use expensive printing equipment that allows for a variety of typefaces, printing styles, colors, and other visual aids. This supermarket style probably works to their disadvantage. When readers see a brightly colored URGENT flagging the face of an envelope, they know immediately that what waits inside is a sales pitch.

Exotically designed sales packages don't capture the attention of busy, intelligent readers. A sober, businesslike appearance to your letter and envelope will establish your credibility and sincerity better than any sales gimmick designed by a commercial outfit.

So take heart if you don't have the services of a high-technology printing firm at your disposal. There are inexpensive ways to print letterheads and envelopes that will reflect favorably on the serious nature of your enterprise. When you ask someone for money, after all, it's wise to appear less than affluent.

Rather than resort to fancy visual devices to attract attention, make your final product look like a real business letter. Whenever possible, include a date, inside address, personalized salutation, and handwritten signature.

If your mailing list comprises hundreds of names, typing each letter by hand is a waste of humanpower and time. The mimeograph machine and other office duplicating machines provide inexpensive ways to mass-produce a letter. Multiple-copy letters, however, do not generally result in a professional-looking product, since the salutation and inside address have to be added after the letter is run off. These additions upset the margins and contrast with the type of the mass-produced letter, detracting from the personalized effect you are after.

Better to find someone among your committee who has access to a memory typewriter or word processor. Someone will have to sit at the machine to insert and extract the letterhead from the typewriter or printer, entering the inside address and salutation on each letter. Meanwhile the letter will type itself. No one will be able to detect that the letter has been mass-produced. This method is best to ensure a neat, personalized appearance.

The appearance of the envelope is equally important. Don't stick labels on the envelope to signal the name and address of the recipient. Type the name and address directly onto the envelope. Omit special signals, such as *Personal and Confidential*, from the envelope. They don't work on the average consumer.

Some volunteer groups omit their names and return addresses from the envelope. If you think it might provide the reader with a motive for not opening the envelope, leave out the name of your organization. A street and city address, on the other hand, is advisable. For a plain envelope hints as much at "seduction" as one that communicates too much.

In the last analysis, you'll need to rely on your own best judgment and the resources available to you when reproducing your letter for a mass mailing. And remember—plan the envelope as carefully as you have organized your letter. You want it to be torn open and its contents digested.

A LETTER TO A POLITICIAN

A depersonalized, promotional-style envelope runs the risk of never being opened. Robin doesn't have to worry about the envelope, however, in the persuasive letter she next writes to her state legislator. Recognizing that state and federal officials welcome letters from their constituents, she modifies her strategy when writing to them.

Since elected officials expect to hear from their voters, Robin spends less time attracting her reader's attention. Nor is she overly concerned about developing a *you attitude*. Furthermore, her letter is (and should be) briefer than her City Hall preservation letter, which is addressed to a wide audience of individuals, many of whom must be wooed into making a commitment. In a legislator-voter relationship, as we all know, it's the legislator who tries to woo the voter.

The reason fewer you-based statements are called for in a letter influencing public policy relates to this legislator-voter relationship. As the writer, you can feel free to talk about your own likes, dislikes, interests, and fears, since you, as voter, may have helped place the reader in a position of power. Local and federal legislators are accountable to their constituents. Your concerns *should* be their concerns.

Looked at another way, it is the voters' responsibility to inform government representatives of their views. Whether or not the legislator will share these views is a moot point. For it has been proven time and time again that lobbying efforts *do* influence the way legislators vote.

Come Across As a Real Person

Don't be afraid to use the personal pronoun *I* in this type of persuasive message. Contrary to what you may have learned in high school English classes, beginning a sentence with *I* is no crime. Just remember that too many repetitions of *I* are boring and may create the impression you're on an ego trip.

Come across as an individual with real ideas and opinions. Legislators are more impressed by constituents who speak from the heart than they are by organized letter-writing campaigns.

That's not to say you can't draw upon hard facts in building an argument or substantiating an opinion. Gather data from the newspapers or TV to back up your ideas. But write your *own* letter rather than use a ready-made model from an organization's campaign literature. Make your message as personal as you can, and write from your home address, not your place of business.

Follow the 3 A's

When writing to your representatives to persuade them to adopt your point of view, follow the 3-A strategy outlined earlier in this chapter: First attract attention, then build your argument, and finally ask for action.

In the opening paragraphs of her letter to Senator Sedita, Robin stimulates interest in her subject by reporting three examples of haz-

ROBIN REDGRAVE
Lincoln Meadows, Apt. 4B
320 Sterling Street
Lyndon City, TX 75212

May 22, 198_

Honorable Ann J. Sedita
The State Senate
Room 509, Legislative Office Bldg.
Fort Apache, TX 75402

Re: Horner/Kopec Bill No. S9500/A7700

Dear Senator Sedita:

Last week three children were hurt at the Lambert Street school
when they stumbled on broken glass scattered on the playground.

A Lyndon County farmer punctured two tractor tires last month
when he ran over a broken beer bottle on Route 59.

In the meantime, the Sterling Street landfill has been running
over with empty bottles and cans.

I'm disturbed every time I pick up the Courier Express to hear
about some new accident caused by the careless disposal of a beer
or soft drink container. So, as a voter in your district, I am
urging you to support the bottle bill that will come before the
Senate next month.

The Horner/Kopec bill, which the House passed last week, will help
make our state a healthy place to live. As the above examples show,
bottles and cans pose real hazards to children, the farming community, and all of us.

Jack Gomez, a state senator from Connecticut, says that since his
state passed a bottle law two years ago the amount of litter in
gutters, alleyways, and countryside has decreased dramatically.

As you know, nine states have adopted a law that encourages people
to take their cans and bottles back to the store instead of to
parking lots, highways, and public parks. Furthermore, these regulations have lightened America's landfills, which are fast running
out of space. Connecticut reports their trash is down by four percent, and Michigan has eliminated 600,000 tons of waste a year.

Beverage bottles and cans now comprise ten percent of all municipal
garbage in the state of Texas. We need to reduce the amount of waste
we bury beneath the ground.

MODEL NO. 8. Letter of persuasion.

Hon. Ann J. Sedita
May 22, 198_
Page 2

We also need to save our energy and natural resources. Our economy today can't afford the wasteful consumption of the past. Let's get those bottles and cans back to the stores so they can be melted down and used again!

Opponents of the bill are saying the new deposit system would cause unsanitary conditions in the stores. They have other arguments against it. I say--Nothing is more unsanitary, dangerous and wasteful than a littered landscape.

Oregon's bottle law has saved taxpayers' money, conserved energy, and created jobs for its citizens. As a state representative, you should want Texas to reap the same benefits.

I urge you to support this bill in committee and on the floor of the Senate. Let's save energy and make Texas a safe, healthy place to live.

Sincerely yours,

Robin Redgrave

(M's) Robin Redgrave

cc: Hon. Douglas H. Shepard
     Hon. Wayne Ellison

ardous conditions in her community. (See Model No. 8.) These local, human interest stories are specific effects of Texas' lack of a bottle regulation and suggest the central motive to which the letter will appeal—the desire for clean, healthy, and sanitary living conditions.

Get to the Point Quickly

Progressing from the specific to the general, Robin, in the fourth paragraph, summarizes her concern for the container problem and quickly gets to her main point and the purpose of the letter: She wants Sedita to vote in favor of the bottle bill. Because legislators (and their assistants) are inundated by constituent letters, it's best not to keep them in suspense too long. State the purpose of your letter early and let them know how you stand on the issue.

Exhibit Your Knowledge

Referring to the introductory examples, the fifth paragraph directly states the central motive. Naming the bill in question, which is also cited in a subject line, Robin informs Sedita she is aware of how the bill fared in the lower house.

Show your reader you know something about what is going on in the legislature. Keep your eyes glued to the newspaper when you are planning a letter like this so you can present facts that convince your reader you are an informed citizen.

Dropping Gomez' name in the next paragraph, Robin now turns to outside authorities to back up her position. Relying on data gathered from newspapers and magazines, she bases this part of her argument on the results of bottle legislation in other states.

Whenever you can, give your beliefs weight by supporting them with some straight facts. Public testimonials to a law's effectiveness will always strengthen an argument.

Be Assertive

As the facts in Robin's letter multiply, her tone of voice becomes more authoritative. Note the tone of the following sentences:

1. *We need to reduce the amount of waste we bury* . . . [from paragraph 8].

2. *We also need to save our energy and natural resources . . .* [from paragraph 9].
3. *Let's get those bottles and cans back to the stores . . .* [from paragraph 9].
4. *As a state representative, you should want Texas . . .* [from paragraph 11].
5. *Let's save energy and make Texas . . .* [from paragraph 12].

The second sentence builds on the simple emotional intensity of the first by repeating its pattern and revealing yet another motive for passing the bill—energy conservation. Becoming bolder in items 3, 4, and 5, she commands her reader's attention by increasing the emotional energy of the appeal.

After exhorting the senator to *get those bottles and cans back to the stores*, Robin introduces one of the opposition's arguments: The bottle bill will create unsanitary conditions in the stores. Ending in strong disagreement with that theory, the tenth paragraph of the letter contains the most aggressively worded statement of her ideas thus far. Its very aggression, however, adds emotional power to the otherwise straightforward presentation of facts around which the argument centers.

Don't be afraid to express your feelings strongly. Just make sure your feelings do not upstage the hard facts of your argument.

Paragraph 11 exposes two new incentives for passage of the bill: It should (1) save the taxpayers money and (2) create new jobs. Notice how reader motives are revealed gradually as the letter picks up emotional speed. By the time the senator nears the end, a number of advantages of the bill have been firmly implanted in her mind.

Senator Sedita, of course, being thoroughly acquainted with both sides of the issue, may not agree with the position you take. Nevertheless, as a voter, you run no risk of alienating her. So long as you have presented your case in a positive way, with logic and enthusiasm, your message will be heard.

End with Power

Repeating the purpose of the letter, the *action* paragraph closes energetically and purposefully by enjoining Senator Sedita to work for the best interests of Texas.

Robin doesn't resort to dull, overused cliches to end her appeal. There is no need to thank the senator for her cooperation and support. She should thank Robin for the sense of responsibility shown in her letter. Neither does Robin press for a response. The purpose of the letter is to affect Sedita's vote, nothing more. Moreover, Robin knows she can expect a response, since most legislators make it a point to answer their constituents' correspondence.

Your letter should, of course, be addressed to the senator or representative from your district. Since your own legislator is but one voice among many, it is wise to also let chairpersons and members of appropriate committees, as well as other government leaders, know your thinking on the issue.

Get Extra Mileage from the Carbon Copy

Most of us don't have the time to write individual letters to each of the people involved with the passage of a law. One way, therefore, to get extra mileage from your letter is to send copies to other legislative members, as Robin has done. Because of their influence on the success or failure of the bill, Governor Doug Shepard and Senate Majority Leader Wayne Ellison are carbon copied. Although you shouldn't carbon copy the whole world in your attempt to make your voice heard, do send your letter to as many parties to the cause as you feel will yield results.

Address your legislators according to protocol by referring to Appendix A. If the legislature is in session, send your letter to the capitol building. If the legislature is on break, mail it to the representative's home address. Address information can be easily obtained from your local library.

A good sense of timing is crucial to the effectiveness of a persuasive appeal to a politician. Your letter must reach its destination before the issue is decided. If you can't find out from the press the date on which the legislative body will vote, get to the reference desk of a library or call your legislator's office for the information. Give that letter plenty of time to be counted!

CHAPTER 7

THE RESUME AND
LETTER OF APPLICATION

SEVERAL YEARS HAVE elapsed since Robin moved to Texas to manage the American Heritage Bookstore, which has flourished under her management. She has become highly visible and respected in her community, not only because she runs Lyndon City's largest bookstore, but because she has been an articulate, effective supporter of the city's development.

Now it is time to move on. Robin's husband, a political science professor, has been offered a job back in New York, their home state, in a city that has recently experienced an economic and cultural revival. Eager to return to a stimulating climate of ice and snow, they ready themselves for a return North, and Robin once again finds herself looking for a job.

Her knowledgeability and interest in the book business guide her naturally toward a position similar to the one she now holds. Because she has experience in college textbook processing as well, she is seriously thinking about working in a college or university setting. A position as bookstore manager for an institution of higher learning is one she is clearly qualified for by her education and work history.

On the other hand, in the course of 25 years she has discovered new talents and capabilities that lead her to reflect on a different, and perhaps more challenging, career prospect. Robin has been an architecture buff for years. Consequently, when Lyndon City stood in danger of losing one of its architectural monuments, she rose to the opportunity to help restore it, uncovering in the process organizational and leadership abilities she never knew she had. With the success of the campaign, she can now lay claim to some distinction as a fundraiser.

Having contributed something valuable to the quality of American life, she feels that her voluntary efforts to preserve a city's historical landmark were more rewarding and self-fulfilling than her work as a bookstore manager. Mulling over this idea, she decides not to shut out the possibility of continuing her public service in similar fundraising projects.

Because she entertains more than one career possibility, Robin needs to be flexible in her approach to a new job. Flexibility, by the way, is a virtue few of us can afford to be without as we search for a job in the 1980s. College degrees today do not represent the easy ticket to employment they once did. Coming out on top in the scramble for jobs in today's market depends less on our educational credentials than on our ability to discover and articulate our acquired skills. Anyone searching for a job today needs to be creative, adaptable, and persistent.

Whether or not you will find the job that is right for you often depends on how carefully you consider your alternatives. Once you have some alternatives in mind, you then need to study how best to pursue them. Assuming you are interested in a professionally oriented position, where resumes and letters are *de rigueur*, you can use one of two approaches—the blind approach or the informed approach. For reasons that will become evident, the informed approach is usually the most effective.

THE BLIND APPROACH

Many people who know which area(s) of the country they want to live and work in barrage companies doing business there with their resumes, hoping to generate several interviews. One of the problems with this method is that you can waste a lot of paper when you don't know if the company you're writing to has an opening in your area of interest or expertise.

Another problem concerns the lack of information you will have at your disposal about the company, its needs, and the requirements of the position for which you are applying. It is always true that applications addressing themselves to specific needs of the company or institution attract the most attention. Yet with the mass-mailing method, you do not usually have enough time to research each of the companies you're interested in. Your resume and letter will therefore lack that individualized feature that constitutes an effective job application package.

This is not to say the blind approach doesn't work sometimes, with or without the candidate's prior knowledge of the company. It's just harder to get it to work, because there's more work to *do*.

Accompanying your probable lack of information about the organization to which you're applying is the problem of whom to send your resume to. There is no standard operating procedure for the hiring of personnel. In some organizations your best bet may be the director or vice president of personnel; in others, the president or chief operating officer is the right person. In most cases, your wisest choice may be the person under whom you would be working or the individual who has the power to hire you. Yet it may be tough to get this information without preliminary correspondence or numerous phone calls. And if you send your resume to the wrong person it may be discarded or misplaced rather than forwarded to someone in the organization interested in your abilities.

I've mentioned that a letter and resume showing knowledge of an organization's needs is more likely to capture a reader's attention. The corollary to this reality is that employers are generally more interested in candidates whose job objectives are clear. If you fail to mention the position you are best qualified for, you will leave your reader up in the air over what to do with your application. At worst, you may create the impression that you are so eager to find employment you are willing to do anything—an impression not likely to spark professional interest in you.

On the other hand, clarification of your career goal or objective may cut you off from other opportunities for which you may be eligible within the company. Unless you are absolutely certain about what you can and want to do for an organization, searching for a job in this "blind" way may not bring you the results you expect.

One final word of warning about this "uninformed" approach to a job. Sending out 50 or so letters at a time requires a great deal of typing. For this reason some job hunters cut corners and resort to a form letter. Form letters are a quick turnoff for most employers, often ending up in the round file. You can hardly expect employers to be interested in you if you can't take the time to write an original letter to them.

For all these reasons, the blind approach decreases your chances of getting an interview, which is your immediate objective in sending out a resume. The resume and letter accompanying it must persuade an employer that you are interested in his or her organization, that you are qualified to work in the organization, and that you can help the organization reach its objectives. This task is difficult when your information about the company is limited. Because the blind method is less effective in generating jobs, this chapter will focus on the *informed* approach.

THE INFORMED APPROACH

The best way to initiate a job interview through the mail is to search for news of an opening for which you are qualified. You will find job opportunities listed in newspapers and in specialized magazines and journals. You may also find out about them by word of mouth. What you need is a lead—a peg to hang your hat on. Once you have found it you can approach the business of finding employment with some confidence.

In advertised positions, employers will often specify, in addition to the job title, the nature of the job, the responsibilities attached to it, and the qualifications they are looking for in a candidate. Knowing the specific requirements of the position is to your advantage; you can use them as a guide in composing your resume and letter. When you know only the title of the opening, you are still a step ahead of the person using the blind approach. All you need to do is use your imagination, and perhaps some outside resources, to figure out the qualifications expected of someone in that job.

Putting together an effective job application package requires careful, strategic planning. How well you plan your strategy depends on how well you have researched *first* the job and/or the company and *second* your abilities and skills.

Research the job and the organization. When the announcement of an opening is well documented, like the *Chronicle of Higher Education* ad on page 93, analyzing the job is relatively simple.

When the information in the ad is skimpy, however, you'll want to do some thinking about the duties attached to the position *and* possibly some outside research. The *Occupational Outlook Handbook*, published by the Bureau of Labor Statistics and available at most public libraries, is a useful source of information about hundreds of jobs in the American marketplace; it is especially valuable to recent college graduates and people making a career change. Published every year, its topics include the working conditions, necessary training, immediate job outlook, and earnings for occupations as diverse and specialized as auto mechanics, law, and radiologic technology.

On the other hand, if you are a seasoned worker with a solid understanding of your work environment, you will already know what is expected of you in a given job. You may then wish to gain some knowledge of the company's operations to help you find a peg on which to hang your resume and letter. Many sources are available to you for this purpose.

For publicly owned industries and service organizations the annual report is an excellent source of information about a company's financial stability, its product lines and services, and its plans for the future. A company's annual report may also target problem areas and plans for expansion, which can give you some ideas on how to approach your subject. A review of earnings and profit figures may also help you decide if the company is right for you. If a company's financial status is less than promising you may expect that opportunities for promotion will be limited and choose not to apply for the job. For a copy of a company's annual report write to the public relations department. You don't have to tell them you're looking for employment.

Other sources of information about a company's history, growth rates, subsidiaries, and products include the *Moody's Manuals*, Dun and Bradstreet's *Million Dollar Directory*, and Standard and Poor's *Register of Corporations*. *Moody's*, which publishes separate books on bank and finance companies, public utilities, and transportation firms, in addition to manufacturing companies, offers the most complete data. The *Million Dollar Directory* and Standard and Poor's *Register* provide less historical data but list the size of the company, its most recent sales and income figures, the nature of the business, and the principal officers.

Not only will background facts on a company be helpful in generating ideas for the letter accompanying your resume, they may help you to formulate intelligent questions to ask during an interview.

Research yourself. The job and company analysis discussed above represents nothing more than an understanding of your audience, a major criterion of all good business writing. In most business situations our own role as writer is pretty clearcut. Except in a letter of persuasion, we generally don't have to think too long or too hard about our own needs and desires. The resume and job letter, however, call for some soul searching. While it may be easy to list your employment and educational background on a piece of paper, it is a real challenge to think of your jobs and schooling in terms of what they might mean to your audience.

To sell yourself to a potential employer, you need to focus on your skills and achievements rather than on your educational degree and past job titles. You might ask yourself just how what you can do will benefit your reader. Employers want to know why you are applying to the organization and what you think you can contribute to its total operation. In other words, they want evidence of your ability to do the job in question. They also want to know what you have to offer that may not be readily available elsewhere. Self-analysis must keep in step with audience analysis.

The remainder of this chapter will reveal how to achieve this balance between self and audience.

RESUME BASICS

Your resume should be designed first. As the less personalized, more objective half of your application package, it can—and in some cases should—be run off by a printer. The resume is a detailed account of the activities, skills, and achievements you've acquired that you judge will be valuable to the kind of job you are seeking. Although resume format and style have experienced an evolution over the last 25 years, many of the job-seeking guides in print today have not caught up with the changes. What follows reflects current trends.*

Make it letter perfect. Important to all good business writing, precision to the last detail is *imperative* in a resume. In addition to

---

*Tom Jackson's *The Perfect Resume* (Garden City: Anchor Books, 1981) is a reasonable guide for those who desire an in-depth treatment of resume writing.

admitting no spelling or grammar errors, the resume should be artfully designed so that headings, job titles, company names, dates, and text follow a consistent pattern pleasing to the eye and easy to read.

Although some people, in the effort to make their resume attract attention, think that a fancy typeface or colored paper is in order, simplicity is the better route. A conventional typeface and high-quality, white bond paper are the least expensive and wisest choices. Some resume-printing firms may try to talk you into a buff- or ivory-colored paper. That's okay, but be sure to type your letter and envelope on the same color paper to achieve a unified look.

Lend visibility to your qualifications by making sure there is a sharp contrast between the ink and the paper in your finished product. That means there should be a fresh ribbon in the typewriter. If your typewriter and/or typing skills are less than the best, have your resume professionally typed. When it is perfectly typed and spaced on the page, a job that involves many trial runs, you will need to decide how to duplicate it.

Professional typesetting is expensive and unnecessary. So choose one of two options: Take it to a printer to be duplicated by the offset process, *or* find a high-quality copying machine in tip-top shape and run it off yourself. Although some resume "experts" advise against the photocopying method, nearly perfect copies that resemble or improve upon the original *can* be achieved. As long as the contrast between ink and paper is sharp and the paper unblemished (no smudges should be visible), your resume will look professional. Don't ever send your original typed resume. You may appear too eager.

Keep it on one page. This is not a hard-and-fast rule, but it's a good one. For one thing, when their openings are publicly advertised, employers are usually bombarded with resumes. Sometimes they read them right away; sometimes their secretaries stack them up for scanning at a later date. In either case, many people dread paperwork. You impose less of a chore on the reviewer of your resume if you keep it short.

For another thing, getting your resume onto one page forces you to record only the most important facts about yourself. Highlighting the relevant, job-oriented data about yourself shows a serious-minded approach to the business of finding a job. It says to an employer *I am a no-nonsense person. I do not pad my resume with irrelevant facts. I want to communicate to you only what I have to offer your organization.*

This advice applies to most business situations today. Years ago, when hiring practices differed, employers expected a standardized format including vital statistics, evidence of marital status and non-job-related interests, and the names of people who could speak for your abilities. As the result of government regulations discouraging discrimination on the basis of sex, race, and age, much of this supplemental information is now left out of a resume.

There are exceptions, of course, to the one-page rule. People in education, for example, whose qualifications for a position may depend on the quality and quantity of their publications, grants, and scholarly presentations, cannot be expected to list all their work on one page. As an insider in your field of expertise, you will undoubtedly be aware of other exceptions. The best I can say is that most readers will appreciate your efforts to limit your resume to one page.

Employers want to know what your accomplishments are and how your skills can achieve results for their company. You can therefore limit your resume to a discussion of your experience and education and *eliminate* the following extraneous information:

- The word *resume*. Anyone looking at it will know what it is. If you use the word *resume* in your letter, don't punctuate it with accent marks; that practice is outdated.
- Age, place of birth, sex, marital status, height, weight, and status of health.
- Religious and political affiliations, unless you are a minister or politician.
- Hobbies and leisure activities.
- All street addresses except your own.
- References. ·
- Salary history.

When you have limited the data about yourself to solid facts about your experience and education, you are ready to decide on a resume format. Although more than two types of resumes are available to you, we will discuss here only the two most commonly used in business—the reverse chronological and functional resumes.*

*For a discussion of other types, see Tom Jackson, *The Perfect Resume*.

THE REVERSE CHRONOLOGICAL RESUME

The reverse chronological resume is the most traditional and conventional of resume formats. At one time it was the only acceptable style for the professional seeking a new job. Although it is still suitable for job seekers in any occupation, today it is used most often in more *traditional* professions—education, the ministry, law, accounting, and the like.

The reverse chronological resume lists your work experience and education in a reverse time sequence; in other words, you work backwards from your most recent job or educational training to your earlier experience. Because the chronological resume highlights dates of employment, job titles, and company names, a prospective employer is able to see at a glance the continuity of your employment history. If you have experienced gaps in your employment background, changed jobs frequently, or held less than impressive job titles, you probably don't want to use this chronological format.

In addition to continuity of employment, a chronological resume emphasizes career development and growth, which makes it suitable when you're looking for a job directly related to your past experience. For this reason Robin uses this format in searching for another bookstore position. Having held two jobs in bookstore supervision and related work in editing, publishing and advertising, she feels confident that the conventional chronological resume (which is easier to write, by the way) will serve her interests well. (See Model No. 9 for Robin's resume in the reverse chronological style.)

Because names of former employers are given top billing on a chronological resume, you may want to use it if you feel these names will add prestige to your qualifications and carry some weight with a prospective employer. It's a form of name dropping, if you will. Just as some employers may be impressed by Harvard or Yale graduates, some may consider a systems analyst from IBM better equipped than an applicant from the Rinky Dink Computer Company. When you are deciding on a resume format, keep in mind that the reviewer of a chronological resume will be drawn initially to the dates, job titles, and places of employment listed there.

The basic components of the chronological resume are the following:

- Name, address, and phone number.

```
                         ROBIN REDGRAVE
                    Lincoln Meadows, Apt. 4B
                       320 Sterling Street
                     Lyndon City, TX 75212
                         (814) 882-9600
```

198_ to   Manager, AMERICAN HERITAGE BOOKSTORE, Lyndon City, Texas
present
           Responsible for total operation of the store, including
           selection of books and gift merchandise; hiring, training
           and supervision of staff of six; inventory, payroll and
           accounting procedures. Determined price strategy and mark-
           up and initiated changes in products to increase sales. As
           liaison between booksellers and the store, maintained
           lines of communication with wholesalers and discovered new
           distribution centers to hold down costs. Managed customer
           relations; prepared and placed local advertisements.

1979-198_ Textbook Supervisor, TRINITY BUSINESS COLLEGE, Milburn, NY

           Processed textbook orders from faculty, placed orders with
           publishers and warehouses, designed procedures for the
           receipt, marking and dispatching of new and used texts,
           supervised annual inventory. In addition, prepared budget
           estimates of sales volume, handled customer complaints, and
           supervised three employees.

1975-1979 Editor, PRENTICE-HALL, INC., Englewood Cliffs, New Jersey

           Researched, wrote, and published study guides about the
           lives and works of Hemingway and Faulkner. Copy edited
           high school English textbooks and assisted in total produc-
           tion process.

1967-1975 Several part-time and temporary positions in advertising,
           public relations, and sales. Assignments included marketing
           research, media analysis, news and copy writing, selling,
           bookkeeping and payroll preparation.

1964-1967 Staff Editor, CIGARETTE ADVERTISING CODE, New York City

           Reviewed and edited radio, TV and print advertising for two
           major tobacco companies, working directly with corporation
           counsel and advertising managers.

EDUCATION B.A. in English, State University College at Fredonia, 1963.
           Minor: Business Administration

           Management Training Seminars, National Association of College
           Stores, held at Oberlin College. 1979, 1980.

           Presently member of National Booksellers Association. Former
           member of National Association of College Stores.

           Fluent in Spanish.

MODEL NO. 9. Reverse chronological resume.

88

- Work history (sometimes referred to as *employment history, work experience, professional experience,* or just *experience*).

- Education (including training seminars and workshops, post-graduate coursework and certification, and conference attendance).

- Other job-related activities or honors (such as membership in professional organizations, awards, honors, and foreign language proficiency).

These are all the facts you need to include on the resume. In composing your first draft, reserve plenty of time to uncover all the functions you've performed in your jobs that apply to your career goal, which, in a chronological resume, should be self-evident.

Type your name, address, and phone number first. These should be centered at the top of the page just as they'd appear in a letter, with each letter of your name capitalized.

If you wish to emphasize your degree or educational background, the education section would appear next. A degree from a prestigious institution, for example, might well be placed early in a resume. As a rule, however, employers searching for experienced people are most interested in a candidate's job history. (This is true unless you're a new graduate looking for an entry-level position, in which case the chronological resume is probably not for you anyway.)

Follow it with your work history. This section should include, in reverse chronological order, all paid employment, including military service duties. Since employers will be drawn to the chronology, avoid showing unaccounted-for intervals of time. If you have too much employment experience to fit on one page, summarize in a brief paragraph employment that is either unrelated to your present career goal or too far back in time to be significant to your present objectives. Summarization is also useful for part-time or temporary positions. Robin, for example, not wanting to show an employment gap, condenses her temporary work from 1967 to 1975, the period during which she was at home with children.

Each of the jobs listed on your resume should contain the following information:

1. *Your job title.* This can be placed before or after the place of employment, depending on where you want the stress to fall. If you want to emphasize it, underline it.

2. *The name and location of the organization.* A street address is not necessary. If you wish to highlight the company name, type it in all caps.

3. *Your dates of employment.* In the interest of space, leave out reference to the month in which you began or finished a job. You probably will not remember it anyway. You can place dates to the left of each job entry, as Robin has done. They can also be typed in after the title and company name and address, which can then begin at the left margin of the paper, allowing more typing space for the job description.

4. *A job description.* In as few words as possible, describe the most important responsibilities or results of each of your jobs, reserving the most space for your most recent position.

As you describe what you did on the job, emphasize those duties and achievements most related to your present job target. Compose the job descriptions carefully. Whenever possible they should reflect your problem-solving ability and the tangible results you achieved for the organization. Potential employers are *very* interested in knowing if you are an individual who can cut costs, increase sales and profits, and solve personnel problems. If you don't get this information on your resume, you need to include it in your letter.

In Robin's description of her work for the American Heritage Bookstore she reports (elaborating on it in her letter on page 97) that she *initiated changes in products to increase sales* and *discovered new distribution centers to hold down costs,* suggesting a serious commitment to the goals of the business.

Be honest. Don't exaggerate your achievements or go on an ego trip. Just show, whenever possible, that you're a person who can get a job done.

Before writing the job description, you must analyze yourself thoroughly. You'll have to do a lot of thinking about what you have done on your jobs and how that work can be translated into a body of skills that will be valuable to a prospective employer. Take the time to describe your skills with precision and clarity.

List your educational qualifications next. The education section should first list the school(s) you have attended. If you attended more than one, start with the latest and work backwards. Each entry in the education section should include the following:

- The degree awarded.
- The name of the institution that granted the degree.
- The date it was awarded.
- Your major, minor, and/or special course of study.
- Honors and awards.

The order in which you arrange these facts depends on which ones you want most visible. If you want your reader to notice first the college from which you received a degree, list the institution first, followed by the degree, the date you received it, and your course of study. If you want the date to be visible within your employment chronology, you can include it at the left margin with the other dates. Proud of her English major from Fredonia State, Robin highlights it by referring to her degree as a B.A. in English.

Include in your education section any honors or awards such as *cum laude, magna cum laude,* and *summa cum laude;* dean's list status; or a high grade point average. Don't overdo it. It would not be necessary, for example, to report that you graduated *magna cum laude,* were a dean's list student, and had a cumulative GPA of 3.6. A simple statement that you graduated *magna cum laude* will take care of all three.

However you decide to arrange your facts, make sure you order them consistently. In other words, follow the same arrangement for each of the institutions you've attended.

After listing your degree(s), you may include in this section your attendance at other schools (making sure you report the nature of the courses or workshops you attended), in-house training seminars (specify if you received a certificate), participation in conferences and conventions related to your profession, and any certificates or licenses that required special training.

Mention other relevant activities or awards. In the interest of conserving space, it is best to include these activities, whenever possible, in your work history or education sections. If you have engaged in many activities outside your business and want to draw attention to them, design a heading that succinctly describes them and place them after either education or work history, whichever seems more appropriate.

Memberships in social or fraternal organizations have no place in a resume unless the work you've done for them transcends their social function. Religious and political affiliations are other qualities of your personal life that have no bearing on your qualifications for a business position. Knowledge of them may prejudice an employer against you.

Activities that may enhance your qualifications in the eyes of an employer include memberships in professional organizations, special company or industry awards or recognition, and the ability to read, write, and speak a foreign language, to mention a few.

Robin has listed her professional affiliations and fluency in Spanish under education. She could, of course, have designed a special heading for the last two items on her chronological resume. But a heading like *Memberships and Special Skills* would have taken more space than was available to her. Notice she has also omitted a heading for her work history.

To get all your qualifications onto one page, use as many short-cuts as possible. Here are some suggestions:

- Consolidate your information into as few categories as possible (ideally just work history and education) to eliminate the need for many headings, which take up space.
- Leave out headings when doing so will not detract from your presentation of data. Generally your first section, whether it be education or work history, can go unannounced. Be sure, however, to signal a transition between your work history and education.
- Use some standard abbreviations. Although you shouldn't abbreviate job titles, words in your job descriptions, or equally important data, some common abbreviations that won't detract from a professional appearance are: the post office abbreviations for states, *Co.* for *Company*, *Inc.* for *Incorporated*, *B.A.* for *Bachelor of Arts*, *B.S.* for *Bachelor of Science*, etc.
- Use decapitated sentences. Instead of beginning the sentences in your job descriptions with *I*, start them off with active verbs

like *supervised, maintained, prepared,* and *designed,* as Robin has done.

- Eliminate linguistic clutter from your job descriptions. (See Chapter 8.)

You must lay out your resume like an artist to make the best use of your space without sacrificing readability. The readability of a resume depends on parallel construction, on the use of capitalization, underlining, and indenting, and on enough white space. (These techniques are discussed in Chapter 8.) Examine carefully the layout of Robin's reverse chronological resume.

After much revising and polishing, Robin's resume is ready to go. As an objective record of her employment history and education, the resume can be used to gain entry to a number of advertised positions.

She now directs her research to all possible channels of communication for jobs related to bookstore management. She makes daily visits to Lyndon City's public library to scan the want ads in New York newspapers and reviews the trade journals that cross her desk. One day she spots this announcement in the *Chronicle of Higher Education:*

UNIVERSITY BOOKSTORE MANAGER

Large city university looking for manager for its $2 million bookstore operation. Applicants must be experienced in textbook ordering and planning, merchandising, and operations supervision. The Manager's responsibilities include:

(1) Administering the textbook operation;
(2) Selecting and ordering gift and supply merchandise;
(3) Coordinating supervisors' functions and overseeing training and supervision of non-management staff of 15;
(4) Establishing and maintaining good relationships with vendors;
(5) Creating and maintaining favorable public relations with students and faculty;
(6) Developing promotional materials to increase bookstore sales.

With a student enrollment of 12,000, William McKinley State University is a grow-ing city university in the heart of downtown Buffalo. The campus, spread out over a 12-block area, is the educational and cultural hub of the city, providing employment opportunities for thousands of Buffalo residents. Buffalo is one hour from Niagara Falls, two hours from Toronto by car, and a half hour from New York City by air. Buffalo's Lake Erie waterfront is considered one of the finest recreational centers in the nation.

Interested applicants should send resume, covering letter and salary requirements to:

M's Shelley Sebouhian, Executive Director
Faculty Student Association
William McKinley State University
256 Seneca Street
Buffalo, NY 14210

Recognizing an excellent opportunity to continue in her present line of work, Robin decides to send her resume to William McKinley State University.

A LETTER TO ACCOMPANY
THE REVERSE CHRONOLOGICAL RESUME

Most guide books on the job search place more emphasis on the resume than on the letter that should accompany it. This is unfortunate. The resume and job letter make up a total package that sells you to a potential employer. Because the letter will be read first, equal attention must be paid to its construction. Since the purpose of the letter is not to *cover* the resume, the phrase *cover letter* is a misnomer. The purpose of the letter is to *stimulate interest* in reading the resume.

Therefore it should be self-contained and attract attention on its own merits. Never send a flat, brief *cover* letter with a resume. As an impersonal, objective report of your experience, the resume may not take into account an individual reader's interest, nor does it always portray you as a special person. Prospective employers want specific information to persuade them you can help the firm reach its objectives.

When you respond to an advertised position you know that your application will be but one of many. And you want yours to stand out from the others. To convince an employer that you are a special candidate for the job, let a little personality shine through.

The main function of the letter is to personalize the resume by *interpreting* it in light of the requirements of the advertised position. How can the skills suggested on your resume be applied to the reader's organization? This is what the reader needs to know. As we discussed earlier in this chapter, the more you know about the company or the job in question, the easier it will be to fit your qualifications into the requirements of the job.

A well documented position announcement, such as the one Robin discovered in the *Chronicle of Higher Education*, will simplify the task of coordinating your skills with what is needed in the new job. William McKinley State University has outlined in detail the responsibilities of the bookstore manager's job, providing a useful guide to the applicant. Not all advertised openings will specify so well the requirements of a position. When they do, however, take advantage of what they tell you about the organization's needs. After reading the ad, Robin knows that William McKinley State wants a person who can direct the ordering and sales of textbooks and other merchandise, supervise a staff, maintain good working relationships with vendors, students and faculty, and develop store promotions. In her letter, therefore, she will show them she can do just that.

Because the job letter should create interest in you as someone who can benefit an organization, it is a letter of persuasion not unlike the letters in Chapter 6, and it should follow the basic strategy of the persuasive letter:

1. Attract attention.
2. Build an argument.
3. Ask for action.

Capture the reader's attention in the first paragraph.   Your opening paragraph should contain four ingredients:

1. It should name the job you're applying for.
2. It should explain where you heard about the opening.
3. It should depict you as an outstanding person for the job.
4. It should show that you want to help the organization.

These four ingredients, skillfully blended, should reveal a strong, positive attitude toward yourself and what you can do for the organization.

Make every sentence in your opener ring with conviction. Avoid dull, bland statements like *I wish to be considered for the position of bookstore manager advertised in last week's* Chronicle of Higher Education. That style is not apt to excite much interest. Don't be flippant either. If you say *I happened to be browsing through the* Chronicle of Higher Education *and noticed you are looking for a bookstore manager*, you will not come across as a serious candidate.

In your opening paragraph (as well as throughout your letter), avoid too many sentences beginning with *I*. Not only is it boring to read a letter in which every sentence starts with *I*, it can also leave the impression that you are self-centered, no matter how hard you show that you can be of service to the reader.

Robin's opening paragraph (Model No. 10) is strong because every word is calculated to attract attention to her specific qualifications for the job. In addition, by stating that her efforts can improve the quality of William McKinley's bookstore, she shows an interest in her prospective employer. By successfully combining the four ingredients, she has developed an opening statement that fits her qualifications to the employer's needs.

Show that you can do the job. A seriousness of purpose, blended with specific details about why she qualifies for William McKinley's opening, is reflected in the body of Robin's letter. With the textbook, merchandising, and operations functions of the job clearly in mind, she clarifies and expands some of the points made in her chronological resume

The two paragraphs in the body of her letter are organized around her two bookstore management positions. The first, interpreting her experience in a college bookstore, shows her competence in textbook processing and personnel training. The second, focusing on her present job, shows that she is equally skilled in handling a store's merchandising and promotional operations.

If you haven't included results in your resume, do so in your letter. Although the resume is a good place to cite the specific results obtained on a job, Robin's intent is to omit these important details from her resume so she can use them to greater advantage in her letter. An application letter should not repeat the information contained in the resume. Save some vital data for your letter to avoid redundancy.

Robin draws attention to the qualifications listed on her resume by highlighting some of her accomplishments in the two bookstore jobs. In her resume entry for Trinity Business College she had listed her duties; in her letter she now stresses results—a new inventory system, a training manual, a healthy relationship with student employees. Similarly, she enhances her job description for the American Heritage Bookstore by revealing one of her achievements there—a 25-percent increase in profit.

Intent to relate her work experience to her reader's needs, Robin incorporates into her argument the *you attitude*. At the end of each of the two paragraphs she expresses her desire to serve William McKinley State University, complementing the closing sentence of her opening paragraph. What she has achieved is a successful balance

ROBIN REDGRAVE
Lincoln Meadows, Apt. 4B
320 Sterling Street
Lyndon City, TX 75212

April 17, 198_

M's Shelley Sebouhian, Executive Director
Faculty Student Association
William McKinley State University
256 Seneca Street
Buffalo, NY 14210

Dear M's Sebouhian:

A strong background in general bookstore management and college
textbook processing, combined with a desire to relocate in my
home state, are my reasons for applying for the Bookstore Manager's
position advertised in last week's Chronicle of Higher Education.
I believe my ability to promote healthy relationships with
customers, vendors, and employees will go a long way toward
making William McKinley's bookstore noticed throughout New York
State.

I became familiar with campus store management as a textbook supervisor for Trinity Business College, where I introduced a new textbook inventory and restocking control system and designed a
training manual for cashiers. In a three-year period I trained over
20 service and stock clerks, most of them students. I believe I can
establish the same rapport with William McKinley's student body that
I did at Trinity.

In addition to processing textbook orders for faculty at one of the
local colleges, I am responsible, in my present job, for all merchandising and operations management. I introduced and implemented a
new brand of merchandise at American Heritage Bookstore, designed an
advertising campaign for it, and obtained a generous allowance from
the manufacturer. This new merchandise increased profits 25 percent over the previous year. To further maximize profits, I
personally monitored and balanced the bookstore stock on a daily
basis. I believe this is important to a successful store business
and would do the same for your operation.

Not included on my resume are a number of references I can send you
after you have reviewed this application.

Please call me at home (814-882-9600) or office (814-973-1000) to
arrange an interview. I look forward to meeting you.

Cordially,

Robin Redgrave

(M's) Robin Redgrave

Enc.

MODEL NO. 10. Letter of application.

between her abilities and her reader's needs, the prime objective of
the job application sales letter.

Offer to provide references.   Most employers, in addition to
checking your previous places of employment, will follow up your
application, either before or after an interview, by contacting people
familiar with your abilities and character. Therefore, have on hand
the names of three to five people who can attest to your honesty, work
habits, and expertise. It is often wise to ask these people to write
letters of recommendation, which you can have sent to your college or
university credentials service. That file of letters can then be mailed
to a number of prospects for employment with the least inconvenience to the person providing the reference.

Many prospective employers, on the other hand, prefer to telephone your references. In any case, when an employer asks for them,
you should have ready the names and addresses of people who will
speak in your favor. Mention briefly in your letter your willingness to
supply these names.

Omit reference to your salary expectations.   Like William
McKinley's advertisement, many invitations to employment request
candidates to provide salary histories or indicate how much salary
they expect to receive. It's best to ignore this request until an
organization is close to making you an offer, at which time you can
negotiate it. By talking salary in a letter, either of two things can
happen. If you shoot too high, you may destroy your chances for an
interview. If you shoot too low, you may get the interview but discover six months into the job that you are underpaid compared to
your co-workers.

The base salary is only one of many financial factors to consider
in deciding whether to accept a position; pension plans, health insurance, and other so-called "fringe" benefits should also influence your
decision. Getting involved with a company's method of remuneration
before you know whether a job is suited to you is probably not in your
best interests.

Ask for an interview.   At the end of your letter remind your
reader of the purpose of your letter—an interview. If you've followed
the advice above by showing you can do the job, you shouldn't have to
beg for one. Avoid those *if clauses* that shed a negative light on all
you've argued for—clauses like *If you feel I am qualified for the posi-*

tion or If I am suited to your firm. (See pages 29–30.) If your letter followed the persuasive strategy, it should be obvious to the reader you are not just a suitable, but an outstanding, candidate.

Without being aggressive, adopt a tone that assumes your readers will be interested in talking to you further and make it convenient for them to do so. It's best not to say you can be available for an interview any time, for it implies your time isn't valuable. If, however, you plan to be in their area at a certain time, let them know. You can even offer to call them when you arrive in town. When you don't foresee a trip to that part of the country, let the employer take the initiative. That's probably the coolest way to go about it anyway. Follow Robin's method. Simply tell them where to reach you, and show you're looking forward to the interview.

Send it early. It's important to send your response to an advertised position as soon as possible. The letters and resumes that reach their destination early in the search process are generally screened first, and you want to ensure that, when an employer begins the interviewing process, your application will be included. If you want it to reach its destination the next day and can invest the extra money, send it by Overnight Express Mail.

If you wish to keep your job search unknown to your present employer, use the *personal and confidential* notation, which will draw attention to your application. (See pages 6–7.) Don't use it, however, unless you have a valid reason for requesting confidentiality. Otherwise the instruction will be regarded as a mere gimmick. An articulate, professionally motivated sales letter needs no gimmicks.

THE FUNCTIONAL RESUME*

The day after she mailed her response to WMSU's announcement, Robin's attention was drawn to a news item in the local paper about an interesting development in Buffalo. She read that the City of Buffalo is currently in political turmoil over the disposition of a building designed by Louis Sullivan. Some monied factions are exerting pressure on the city government to let them tear down the building in the name of progress. The city fathers, on the other hand, want to initiate

---

*Since my advice on the functional resume and letter is tangential to discussion of the chronological resume and letter, you need to have read the earlier portions of this chapter before proceeding.

a drive to raise money for the building's restoration. The last sentence of the article mentioned they are looking for someone to direct the campaign.

As a devotee of Sullivan's work Robin greets the news with dismay, tempered by her enthusiasm for the proposed restoration. Thinking of the long hours spent on the City Hall preservation project, she recalls her feeling of satisfaction when Lyndon City reached its campaign goal and turned away the out-of-town investment group. Wouldn't it be exciting to triumph again! Can she do it? Can she market herself as an experienced fundraiser?

Certainly not with the chronological resume she designed, which describes only her paid employment. That resume didn't even mention her voluntary community work. She needs a resume that will call attention to her capabilities in a line of work different from the one she is now engaged in. So, sitting down at the drawing board once again, she begins work on a functional resume.

The functional resume organizes your experience by function rather than by employment. Whereas in a reverse chronological resume job titles, places of employment, and dates are stressed, in a functional resume they are subordinated to skills. When the work you're aspiring to is unrelated to your present or previous paid employment, you will be wise to construct a functional resume to focus on your skills and abilities.

In a functional resume you don't need to link your skills with the specific jobs in which you exhibited or learned them. A functional resume demonstrates to a potential employer that you can do the job in question because you have the expertise. Where you got it is a secondary matter.

For this reason the functional resume is a good choice for people changing careers. If you're entering the professional job market for the first time, trying to break into a new career, or returning to the working world after an absence, consider using a functional rather than a chronological format. All that we have said earlier in this chapter about analyzing yourself in terms of your perception of an organization's needs applies here. Identify those skills and competencies that you know are vital to the kind of work you wish to pursue. Then talk about them.

College graduates embarking on their first full-time professional jobs may be wise to adopt the functional format, since they are undergoing a transformation from student to professional. Many new college graduates have only part-time and summer employment to detail on a chronological resume. For the most part these jobs (like fast-food and maintenance work) are in the service industries and require no special skills. A resume highlighting part-time and temporary work at McDonald's, Kroger's and a summer day camp, for example, will say very little about a candidate's potential as a professional. A functional resume describing specific skills acquired and practiced in these jobs will say more.

Categorize your qualifications by function. After centering your name, address, and phone number at the top of the page, you're ready to talk about the functions in which you've developed proficiency. Reflect on your experiences and accomplishments in employment, community work, governance activities, and internships. Write them down. Then group them according to function. You should be able to identify at least two basic skills or areas of involvement. These will become headings in your resume.

For example, you may wish to classify your skills by identifying the fields in which you've developed expertise, such as construction, aviation, architecture, social work, computer programming, civil engineering, or real estate. Under each of these headings you can then describe the most important functions performed.

Another method is to formulate headings that talk directly to the reader about your abilities, the method Robin has used. (See Model No. 11.) Think of your past performance in terms of basic skills like these:

- Supervisory and Management Ability
- Accounting Skills
- Writing and Editing Experience
- Materials Handling Skills
- Administrative Ability
- Interpersonal Communications Skills
- Retailing Experience
- Market Research Skills
- Product Development Experience
- Financial Planning and Development Skills

This list is by no means exhaustive. You will have to come up with captions that fit you.

```
                         ROBIN REDGRAVE
                    Lincoln Meadows, Apt. 4B
                       320 Sterling Street
                      Lyndon City, TX 75212
                         (814) 882-9600
```

SALES AND FUNDRAISING EXPERIENCE:

- Developed and ran promotional campaign as chair of preservation committee for Texas landmark, achieving goal of over $1 million.

- Identified, implemented, and advertised new brand of bookstore merchandise, resulting in 25% increase in profit.

- Established wage incentives for bookstore personnel, which increased total sales for two consecutive years.

- Sold Avon products to over 400 clients, grossing $12,000 one year.

ADMINISTRATIVE ABILITY:

- Coordinated all staff activities and office procedures for City Hall Preservation Committee, Lyndon City, Texas.

- Developed, coordinated and supervised all accounting, budget, and payroll records for large bookstore operation.

- Hired, trained, and supervised personnel in sales, inventory, and accounting procedures.

RESEARCH AND WRITING SKILLS:

- Composed all correspondence for City Hall Preservation campaign, which reached 80% of city residents by mail; compiled and wrote up data for monthly progress reports to the Committee.

- Conducted market research, wrote news releases and advertising copy (in Spanish and English), and planned media campaign for international manufacturer based in New York City.

- Researched and wrote study guides on Hemingway and Faulkner.

```
WORK HISTORY:  198_ to    GENERAL MANAGER
               present    American Heritage Bookstore, Lyndon City
               1979-198_  TEXTBOOK SUPERVISOR
                          Trinity Business College, Milburn, NY
               1975-1979  EDITOR, Prentice-Hall, Inc.
               1967-1975  Part-time/temporary work in advertising,
                          public relations, and sales.
               1964-1967  EDITOR, Cigarette Advertising Code, NYC

EDUCATION:  B.A., 1963.  Major: English  Minor: Business Administration
                         State University College at Fredonia
```

MODEL NO. 11. Functional resume.

102

Your skills categories should be arranged in descending order of importance. In other words, place the strongest or most relevant skills category first on your resume. Similarly, the most important functions performed within each skills area should appear first.

To attract attention to her experience as a fundraiser, Robin places *Sales and Fundraising Experience* in first position on her functional resume. The first entry under that heading summarizes her work for the City Hall Preservation Committee. In second and third position are two of her major accomplishments for the American Heritage Bookstore, followed by her achievement as an Avon salesperson during a period when she worked at home. Each of these accomplishments is described concisely in half sentences that begin with verbs denoting resourceful action—*developed, ran, identified, implemented, established, sold.*

In the second category, *Administrative Ability*, Robin describes her management and supervisory functions as chair of the preservation committee in the first entry, since she wants to draw attention to her fundraising experience. The following entry reflects her work for the Lyndon City bookstore, while the third takes into account her duties at both bookstore jobs.

Again, under *Research and Writing Skills*, the category third in importance in Robin's judgment, she highlights the preservation campaign work by placing it first. Because her research and writing activity at the bookstores was usually routine, Robin digs deeper into her past experience to deal with some of her part-time and temporary assignments in advertising, public relations, and publishing.

In summary, Robin has invented headings that speak strongly to her ability to perform the functions of a professional fundraiser. She has used vivid action verbs to introduce the hard facts and figures that promote her skills as a fundraiser. Not attempting to show continuity of employment or career development, she has addressed herself only to those functions of her experience that relate to the new career objective she has set for herself.

Don't restrict your skills to employment functions. Remember that one of the virtues of the functional resume is the opportunity it gives you to display skills you've acquired from your total experience. Volunteer work, community involvement, and temporary employment are areas of your total experience that can enhance your qualifications for a specific job. Students applying for an entry-level job should also recognize that the skills acquired in coursework, intern-ships, and campus governance activities should be of more interest to a potential employer than some of the functions associated with paid employment in the unskilled labor market.

Use bullets to set off each function.   To make your functional resume visually interesting, place a symbol (known as a *bullet*) in front of each of the functions within your broad categories. Bullets can be circles, squares, arrows, or other signs that highlight each item in a vertical list. The easiest bullet to construct on a typewriter is the circle.* Simply type a lower-case *o* (slightly raised from the line) one or two spaces before the first line of each entry, as Robin has done. (See Model No. 11.) You can then fill the circle in with black ink before you have the resume run off.

Briefly outline your work history.   The most important ingre-dient of the functional resume is a thorough, succinct description of the functions you can perform. This should take up most of the page. Since most employers like or need to know where you have worked, follow your skills identification with a brief rundown of your places of employment. Leave out job descriptions, since you have cataloged your strong points within the functional categories.

Your job title, the name of each organization (with the location, if you have space), and dates of employment should be arranged in reverse chronological order.† In her functional resume (Model No. 11) Robin arranges her employment facts as she did on her chronolog-ical resume, eliminating the job descriptions and crowding the items somewhat to conserve space.

Place your educational degree(s) last.   List, in reverse chro-nological order, the institutions at which you obtained degrees. If you have space limitations, only the degree, date, and institution are necessary. If you attended college(s) without receiving a degree, you may mention it here or refer to the experience in your skills section. Similarly, relevant school activities or awards may be more appropri-ately included as accomplishments in your skills section. Remember that the emphasis of a functional resume is on the functions you can or have performed. Your work history and education sections should

*Asterisks do not make good bullets because they are commonly used as signals for footnotes.

†See page 90 for advice on how to arrange these facts.

take a back seat to these functions in terms of the amount of space allotted to them.

A LETTER TO ACCOMPANY THE FUNCTIONAL RESUME

Now that she has a resume usable for entry into a new line of work, Robin reflects on how to introduce it in a letter. First, however, she must decide to whom to send the letter. The report on Buffalo's Sullivan building in the *Lyndon City Courier Express* was a news release, not a formal job announcement. It didn't mention the names of any individuals involved in the project. Lacking this information, she determines that the mayor of the city must be in communication with the organizers of such an important campaign. Why not write to him, asking him to pass her application on to the appropriate parties?

Once she has identified her reader, Robin can proceed to strategy. Since Mayor Pulaski hasn't invited her request for an interview, she decides the direct style would not suit her interests. Surmising that the mayor has a vested interest in the preservation project, she decides to gain his attention by talking about it, delaying the intent of the letter to the third paragraph. (See Model No. 12.)

The strategy Robin employs is the strategy of a typical letter of persuasion. (See Chapter 6.) Her goal is to create for her readers strong motives for them to interview her. So she tells her reader(s) that she is a native Buffalonian, that she has experience *and* success in raising money for the restoration of architectural landmarks, and that she has contacts in government and the community that will serve Buffalo's interests.

The peg on which she hangs all of this is, of course, the news item from the *Lyndon City Courier Express*. A little mild flattery and a *you viewpoint* get the letter off to a bright start. To encourage the mayor and other interested parties, Robin tells him of Lyndon City's success in a similar project, evincing her enthusiasm for the Buffalo campaign. Then she states her desire to conduct the Buffalo campaign, detailing her work in Texas to supplement the information on her resume and attract attention to it. Politely requesting Pulaski to inform the committee of her credentials, she accommodates the reader by offering to travel at her own expense, proof of her high level of interest in the job. The closing gesture of *Best wishes and personal regards* reinforces the empathy sustained throughout.

ROBIN REDGRAVE
Lincoln Meadows, Apt. 4B
320 Sterling Street
Lyndon City, TX 75212

home phone: 814-882-9600   office phone: 814-973-1000

April 20, 198_

Honorable Chester T. Pulaski
Mayor of Buffalo
City Hall
Buffalo, NY 14220

Dear Mayor Pulaski:

You'll be pleased to learn that Buffalo's latest preservation campaign has made the news in Texas. The April 17 Lyndon City Courier Express disclosed your upcoming project to save the Hancock Building from a demolition crew. I read this news with special interest, for two years ago another one of Louis Sullivan's buildings was in danger of being replaced by a steel and concrete parking garage.

I was chair of the committee formed to avert this disaster and preserve the work of one of our greatest American architects. Our campaign was successful. Today Lyndon City's Sullivan landmark, old City Hall, is being renovated into office space for the business community.

This brings me to the purpose of my letter. In the fall my husband and I are returning to Western New York State. I am very interested in conducting your campaign to restore Buffalo's Hancock Building and would like to be considered for the job.

We ran Lyndon City's preservation project on a very low budget, working out of offices provided by the city. With two clerical assistants, I mailed letters to thousands of residents, planned and coordinated promotional parties and information sessions, and developed grant proposals to federal and state agencies.

My knowledge of Sullivan's work, my established contacts with architects and historians interested in the preservation of 19th-century buildings, and my familiarity with Buffalo (having been born and raised there) will all, I feel, contribute toward the success of your efforts to preserve the Hancock Building.

MODEL NO. 12. Letter of application.

Mayor Pulaski
April 20, 198_
Page 2

I will therefore appreciate your sending this letter and resume to
the committee in charge of the campaign so it can get in touch with
me for an interview. Given a few days' notice I am willing to fly
to Buffalo at my own expense. I will also be happy to send along
the names of people you can contact for references.

Best wishes and personal regards.

Sincerely,

Robin Redgrave

Robin Redgrave

Enc.

When she began this undertaking Robin regarded it as a shot in the dark, since her information about the job was limited. In the process of composing the resume and letter, she has convinced herself that she is the ideal person for the job. She feels confident, when she reaches the end of her letter, that she will get an interview. That is perhaps the final and only test for the effectiveness of a persuasive appeal. If by the time you've finished you've convinced yourself, you've probably done all you can do.

Of course, she can't just sit back and wait for responses to her two letters of application. Many more letters will be written in the upcoming weeks. Yet her efforts so far have produced two viable resumes that answer to her alternative career goals. Her task now is to find the leads, to resourcefully and energetically promote her abilities, and to prepare for the interviews that will inevitably follow.

CHAPTER **8**

STYLE

BECAUSE VERBAL PRECISION is vital to successful communications, you must edit your letters carefully to sustain your readers' interest in your message and get them acting on it. In this book we have stressed that writing is a three-stage process. We have seen Robin devote much of her letter-writing time to prewriting—thinking about her audience and the purpose of her communication. When her letters are written, she spends an equal amount of time revising and polishing them. This chapter will cover the principles Robin follows to ensure that her message will be heard.

THE WORD

Choose the Plain Word over the Fancy

Always strive to use words that are quickly understood and retained. People who avoid the common, ordinary word or expression, whether purposely or unconsciously, are deceiving their readers and possibly themselves. Some people write in a windy, pretentious way because they *are* windy and pretentious. If you're one of these people, lift your head out of the sand and see yourself as you are. Other business writers get tangled up in high-flown, fancy words because they can't figure out what they're supposed to say. If that's your problem, re-think the purpose and audience of your letter.

Lawyers, government people, and administrators of all kinds are the main perpetrators of word fraud. Some of us are so used to seeing sentences like the following issuing from high places that we come to accept them as good English:

> *However, the exigencies of our present economic condition pose unsettled questions in regard to the preservation of the Sullivan Building.*

This sentence illustrates what has come to be known as *gobbledy-gook, bureaucratese,* or *Corp Speak.* The sentence is obscure because the words draw attention to themselves instead of to the idea behind them. Robin said the same thing in simple language: *Hard times are upon us, however.*

Common, everyday words wear the best. This sentence is stodgy and dull:

> In addition, I *shall* be *pleased* to *submit* to you the names of *individuals* who will *supply* you with references.

Not only does this sentence contain more words than it needs for the simple idea expressed, but it suggests the writer is a little stuffy. The words in italics are loftier than they need to be. When strung together, they result in a vision of the writer as a holier-than-thou Victorian merchant or schoolmarm. *Shall* is no longer used by Americans in conversation; *pleased* is too reserved; *submit* implies you're sending portentous legal documents instead of a simple list of names; *individuals* is a stiff, impersonal word for people who are going to speak in your behalf; and *supply* suggests these people all work in shipping departments. This simpler version is more sane:

> *I will also be happy to send along the names of people you can contact for references.*

Here are more examples of how plain, ordinary words make for friendlier, less formal prose:

- This group plans to *obliterate* the *edifice* and build an apartment complex.
  (Substitute *tear down* for *obliterate* and *building* for *edifice*.)
- Horizon Publishing Company has recently experienced operational difficulties at its *printing facility*.
  (Substitute *plant* for *printing facility*.)
- We worked out of *office facilities* provided by the city.
  (Substitute *offices* for *office facilities*.)
- We therefore *propose* you send us the names and addresses on your gift list.
  (Substitute *suggests* for *propose*.)
- *Longevity* is not the only *determinant* of a landmark's value.
  (Substitute *age* for *longevity*, convert *determinant* to *determine*, and write: *Age alone does not determine a landmark's value*.)

Make Your Verbs Strong

Action verbs give life to sentences. Some verbs—like *is, are, was, have*, and *had*—are low in action. When linked with nouns and adjectives, these verbs draw attention to the nouns and adjectives instead of to the action expressed. Notice the difference between these two sentences:

- We *are* sincerely *appreciative* of your interest in working for the American Heritage Bookstore.
- We sincerely *appreciate* your interest in working for the American Heritage Bookstore.

The second sentence is better because the verb is stronger.

An addiction to nouns and adjectives over solid, action verbs makes for heavy, wordy prose. Try to rely on verbs as much as possible, especially when your sentences are long to begin with. Study these two sentences:

- *I have the belief that* my ability to promote healthy relationships with customers, vendors, and employees will go a long way toward m`aking William McKinley's bookstore noticed throughout New York State.
- Now we *are in need of* civic and business leaders like you to come forward and assist in this great undertaking.

When simple verbs are substituted for the italicized words, the writer speaks more convincingly:

> I *believe* my ability to promote healthy relationships . . . We *need* civic and business leaders like you . . .

If you keep your verbs at a high energy level, you'll avoid awkward sentences like this one:

> Eighty-five years ago *there was a contrast between* Sullivan's steel frame and vertical lines and the classic Greek and Roman styles of his contemporaries.

The idea in this sentence has been watered down by the unnecessary words. Let the verb carry the weight of the action and write it like this:

> Eighty-five years ago Sullivan's steel frame and vertical lines *contrasted* with the classic Greek and Roman styles of his contemporaries.

Substitution of the verb *contrasted* reduces the sentence by four words, creating a more proficient expression of the idea.

A quick look at one of Robin's resumes will illustrate how verbs pack power. Her job descriptions, you'll remember, relied on strong verbs:

- *Managed* customer relations . . .
- *Processed* textbook orders . . .
- *Prepared* budget estimates . . .
- *Researched, wrote,* and *published* study guides . . .
- *Reviewed* and *edited* radio, TV, and print advertising . . .

Add the subject *I* to the verbs and you have a clear, visual picture of the writer's accomplishments.

In addition to presenting a clearer picture to the reader, strong verbs eliminate word clutter and make your sentences read more smoothly. The more unneeded words you eliminate from your sentences, the better the quality of the idea:

I *was* the *major facilitator* in the *development* of grant proposals to federal and state agencies.

The idea in this sentence has been diluted. Eliminate the garbage and you reveal a person with firm beliefs:

I *developed* grant proposals to federal and state agencies.

Study these weak sentences and their translation into more robust statements:

- Opponents of the bill *are coming out with statements claiming that* the new deposit system would cause unsanitary conditions in the stores.
  (**Change to:** Opponents of the bill *are saying* the new deposit system would cause unsanitary conditions in the stores.)
- Furthermore, these regulations *have been responsible for lightening* America's landfills.
  (**Change to:** Furthermore, these regulations *have lightened* America's landfills.)
- I *had the responsibility of introducing* a new textbook inventory and restocking control system.
  (**Change to:** I *introduced* a new textbook inventory and restocking control system.)

Very often you can firm up your sentences by substituting a verb phrase for a noun phrase:

Let's all pull together *for the maintenance of* our community's reputation.
(**Change to:** Let's all pull together *to maintain* our community's reputation.)

Sometimes you can even strike out whole phrases to strengthen the verb:

Today Lyndon City's Sullivan landmark, old City Hall, *is in the process of being renovated* into office space for the business community.

(**Change to:** Today Lyndon City's Sullivan landmark, old City Hall, *is being renovated* into office space for the business community.)

Remove Redundant Words

In the last sentence we were able to remove four words (*in the process of*) for a more efficient sentence. Making every word count is one of the main goals in editing. Suppose you ran across a sentence like this:

The loss of the Sullivan building will deprive Lyndon City of a major part of its historical heritage.

Looks all right, doesn't it? The verb is active and the words plain enough. But wait a minute. What does the writer mean by *historical heritage*? Isn't a sense of history part of the meaning of *heritage*? *The American Heritage Dictionary* defines *heritage* as *something other than property passed down from preceding generations; legacy; tradition*. Therefore, what we receive and retain from our ancestors results from our past and our past *is* our history. The word *historical* in this instance is redundant.

Redundancies easily slip by us as we write, probably because they've become so much a part of our speech patterns. We should try to rid ourselves of them on paper, however. Guard against using words that are implied in another. Here are some common redundancies. (The superfluous word is in italics.)

actual experience	We wouldn't refer to it as an experience if it didn't *actually* happen.
valuable asset	Though some assets are more valuable than others, all have value or we wouldn't call them assets.
critical emergency	All emergencies are critical.
adequate enough	There are no degrees of adequacy.
completely eliminated	The word *elimination* indicates completeness.
final completion	Completions are always final.
general consensus	*Consensus* means general opinion.

consensus *of opinion*	ditto
important essentials	All essentials are important.
mutual cooperation	There is no cooperation without mutuality.
assemble *together*	*Assemble* means putting *together*.
combine *together*	Same problem.
a variety of *different* people	*Variety* contains the idea of difference.
complete monopoly	Monopoly always means *complete* control.
necessary prerequisite	A prerequisite is something that's needed.

Other widespread redundancies occur in the form of *wasteful couplets*. The following sentence contains a wasteful couplet:

Beverage bottles and cans now comprise ten percent of all municipal *garbage and waste* in the state of Texas.

It should be evident that all garbage is waste, and that one of those words can be eliminated without losing any essential information. Similarly—I introduced *and implemented* a new textbook inventory system—can very well do without the italicized words. We assume that the writer's act of introducing the system included its implementation.

Here are more wasteful couplets:

- I am *anxious and eager* to help you with the Sullivan campaign.
- Lyndon City residents understand the *value and importance* of Walter Hampton's new book.
- We need your *help and assistance* next year.
- Please *collect and gather together* all the facts on Buffalo's Hancock Building.
- I will *communicate with you and write you* at your business address.

Watch for needless repetition from one sentence to another:

> I became familiar with campus store management as a textbook supervisor for *a college in upstate New York*. At *Trinity Business College* I introduced a new textbook inventory and restocking control system and designed a training manual for cashiers.

We lose no important information and clarify the message when we refer to the college once instead of twice:

> I became familiar with campus store management as a textbook supervisor at Trinity Business College, where I introduced . . .

Wipe Out Prepositional Deadwood

The overuse of prepositions can also interfere with the clarity of an idea. This sentence stumbles before it gets to the end:

> A farmer *in Lyndon County* punctured two tires *on his tractor, during the last month* when he ran *over a broken beer bottle, on Route 59*.

The sentence is smoother when three of the prepositional phrases are eliminated:

> A Lyndon County farmer punctured two tractor tires last month when he ran over a broken beer bottle on Route 59.

In the first draft of her City Hall preservation letter, Robin wrote:

> The national landmarks *of* our country exist *to* inform us *about* the great historical and cultural events *of* the past.

After studying the tone and sense of this sentence she removed all the prepositions for this less burdensome, crisper model:

> Our national landmarks help us understand our history.

When prepositions are sprinkled too freely into your prose the idea behind the words diminishes. Look what happens in the next sentence when three of the prepositions are wiped out:

Original:

- This new line *of* merchandise resulted *in* a 25-percent increase *in* profit *over* the previous year.

Improved:

- This new merchandise increased profits 25 percent over the previous year.

Notice we've changed *resulted in* to *increased* to eliminate the needless extra noun.

Tightening up your sentences really pays. When you stop beating around the bush, you will come across as a person who firmly believes what you say.

When you choose the one-word substitute over the prepositional phrase, you get to your point quicker. Examine the following list of prepositional deadwood.

Deadwood	*Change to:*
in the amount of	for
in the effort to	to
for the purpose of	for
in order to	to
due to the fact that	because, since
in the event that	if
for the reason that	because, since
during the time that	while
in regard to	about
in close proximity to	near
with reference to	about, concerning
in the near future	soon
at the present time	now
in the majority of cases	usually
of considerable magnitude	large
at a rapid rate	rapidly

Abandon Needless Pronouns

The pronouns *who* and *which*, when used to introduce relative clauses, often weight down a sentence and produce a clumsy effect. In the following examples, the improved version flows better:

Original:

- They sent the September bill to Mr. and Mrs. Richard Graf, *who are* the former owners of the property.

Improved:

- They sent the September bill to Mr. and Mrs. Richard Graf, the former owners of the property.

Original:

- Barbara Wardzinski, *who is* Horizon's sales manager, telephoned to explain that her press is working overtime to reprint the covers.

Improved:

- Barbara Wardzinski, Horizon's sales manager, telephoned to explain that her press is working overtime to reprint the covers.

Original:

- At the closing I turned over to Oil City Savings and Loan, *which is* the bank holding my mortgage, $1,142.50 plus the late payment fine of $75.87.

Improved:

- At the closing I turned over to Oil City Savings and Loan, the bank holding my mortgage, $1,142.50 plus the late payment fine of $75.87.

Original:

- Your order for the above book, *which you* placed last month when you were in our store, is, as always, greatly appreciated.

Improved:

- Your order for the above book, placed last month when you were in our store, is, as always, greatly appreciated.

Eliminate Unnecessary "That's"

Be ever on the alert for words that impede the natural flow of your sentences. The word *that* often encumbers a sentence by interrupting the flow of ideas. Study this sentence by reading it aloud:

> Oil City Savings and Loan Association has suggested *that* I write you about a charge for late payment of school taxes.

Delete the word *that* and your idea lightens up and stands out better:

Oil City Savings and Loan Association has suggested I write you about a charge for late payment of school taxes.

I'm not suggesting the word *that* can always be deleted. Sometimes it detracts from the flow to remove it, as in the following sentence:

Just today, Barbara Wardzinski, Horizon's sales manager, telephoned to explain *that* her press is working overtime to reprint the covers.

Removal of *that* in this case might tamper with the clarity of the sentence. Study each sentence for rhythm and clarity before deciding whether the word *that* is unnecessary. Here are more sentences in which removal of the word *that* improves the sound and sense:

Original:
- Enclosed is a copy of the bill *that* I paid under protest.
Improved:
- Enclosed is a copy of the bill I paid under protest.
Original:
- I was unaware *that* the City would not be sending the tax bill directly to Oil City Savings.
Improved:
- I was unaware the City would not be sending the tax bill directly to Oil City Savings.
Original:
- Knowing *that* you need these books for Christmas presents, we immediately reshipped them to Horizon's warehouse and requested a duplicate order.
Improved:
- Knowing you need these books for Christmas presents, we immediately reshipped them to Horizon's warehouse and requested a duplicate order.
Original:
- Opponents of the bill are saying *that* the new deposit system would cause unsanitary conditions in the stores.
Improved:
- Opponents of the bill are saying the new deposit system would cause unsanitary conditions in the stores.

Don't Leave "This" in a Vacuum

To achieve clarity, avoid words that are ambiguous in their contexts. One of the biggest deterrents to clarity is careless use of the pronoun *this*. Can you interpret the second of these sentences?

> The accountant told a funny story. This made her boss laugh.

Not being acquainted with the accountant in question we are hard put to know whether her boss was laughing at the story, her manner of telling it, or the accountant herself. The author's meaning is shrouded in mystery.

This is a vague, imprecise word that leaves your sentences open to misinterpretation. Study the following paragraph:

> The Horner/Kopec bill, which the House passed last week, will help make our state a healthy place to live. As the above examples show, *this* poses real hazards to children, the farming community, and all of us.

In the above example the word *this* is unexplained in the context of the paragraph. To understand what the writer means, you have to go back to the earlier paragraphs and infer that the hazards under discussion here are *carelessly discarded bottles and cans*. (See page 74.) If the reader is reading quickly she may easily misconstrue your meaning and interpret *this* to refer to the Horner/Kopec bill. Don't confuse your readers or leave any doubt in their minds about your ability to write a coherent sentence.

In other words, if what *this* refers to is not immediately clear, your reader will be grateful if you add a noun to it. The word *this* is imprecise in the next example:

> Just today, Barbara Wardzinski, Horizon's sales manager, telephoned to explain that her press is working overtime to reprint the covers. *This* will reach us on December 27.

Obviously it's not the covers that will arrive at the bookstore on December 27; Robin intends to say that the *new books* or *new shipment* will arrive that day. Say exactly what you mean.

A solitary *this* usually refers to a person, thing, or idea mentioned in a previous sentence. For verbal precision, add a noun to complete the thought.

>   *Don't Say:*
> - Please let us know how we should handle *this*.
>   *Say:*
> - Please let us know how we should handle *your order*.
>   *Don't Say:*
> - We sincerely appreciate your interest in *this*.
>   *Say:*
> - We sincerely appreciate your interest in *working for the American Heritage Bookstore*.
>   *Don't Say:*
> - If *this* is not satisfactory, may we suggest an alternative?
>   *Say:*
> - If *this arrangement* is not satisfactory, may we suggest an alternative?

Use "It" Not "They" for Collective Nouns

A common verbal error in business writing is the use of the plural pronoun *they* (and the adjective *their*) when referring to a group or organization. In America any company, government, agency, council, committee, or other organization of people is considered a single unit. Consequently, these words and others, like *management, corporation*, and *division*, always take singular verbs. To be consistent, you must also use the word *it* or *its* in substituting for the word itself, as in the following examples:

>   *Wrong:*
> - Horizon Publishing Company has recently experienced operational difficulties at *their* plant.
>   *Right:*
> - Horizon Publishing Company has recently experienced operational difficulties at *its* plant.
>   *Wrong:*
> - I will therefore appreciate your sending this letter and resume to the committee in charge of the campaign *so they* can get in touch with me.

Right:

- I will therefore appreciate your sending this letter and resume to the committee in charge of the campaign so *it* can get in touch with me.

Wrong:

- Were you here in 1942 when Lyndon City State University opened *their* doors to us?

Right:

- Were you here in 1942 when Lyndon City State University opened *its* doors to us?

Similarly, cities and states are treated as single units:

Wrong:

- Many architectural historians are standing by to see if Lyndon City has the courage to fight for *their* most famous architectural landmark.

Right:

- Many architectural historians are standing by to see if Lyndon City has the courage to fight for *its* most famous architectural landmark.

Wrong:

- Oregon's bottle law has saved taxpayers' money, conserved energy, and created jobs for *their* citizens.

Right:

- Oregon's bottle law has saved taxpayers' money, conserved energy, and created jobs for *its* citizens.

THE SENTENCE

Avoid "Dick and Jane" Sentences

In the primary grades, when we were learning to read and write, we read sentences like these: *Dick sees the ball. Jane sees the ball. Dick and Jane run after the ball. Spot sees the ball. Spot catches the ball.* These short, simple sentences suit the small vocabulary and limited sentence patterns of the early reader.

As we progress in the language, however, our attention span widens, we are able to conceptualize better, and our sentence patterns become more complex. An adult might decide to put the ideas together like this: *As Dick and Jane are running after the ball, Spot catches it.* As adults we can combine and see relationships among the ideas in those sentences and express those ideas in a way that visualizes them better for the reader.

Short, choppy sentences starting with the subject followed by the verb are not conceptually interesting to the sophisticated adult reader. They weaken the attention span and take longer to digest. Study these sentences:

1. I never received a bill for the school tax.
2. I am told it was issued late in September.
3. I was surprised when I received a bill for $1,142.50 plus the late payment fine of $75.87.
4. I received this bill in January.
5. I have since talked with the city tax collectors.
6. They told me they sent the September bill to Mr. and Mrs. Graf.
7. Mr. and Mrs. Graf are the former owners of the property.

The sentences are boring because they're all in the same style—first the subject, then the verb. Five of them start with *I*. Although the facts are complete, the choppy sentences make it hard for the reader to see how the facts relate to one another.

Here is the way an experienced writer might put together the same facts:

1. Because I never received a bill for the school tax, which I am told was issued late in September, I was surprised when, in January, I received a bill for $1,142.50 plus the late payment fine of $75.87.
2. I understand now, after talking with the city tax collectors, that they sent the September bill to Mr. and Mrs. Richard Graf, the former owners of the property.

Although this paragraph contains the same facts, they've been combined so the reader gets a clearer mental picture of the action. Here is how the original sentences were reworked:

1. The idea in the first sentence of the earlier paragraph has been subordinated to the idea in the third sentence.
2. The second sentence has been turned into a clause modifying *bill for the school tax* from the first sentence.
3. The fourth sentence is transformed into a prepositional phrase and imbedded in the third sentence.
4. The fifth sentence has been subordinated to the sixth.
5. The seventh sentence is transformed into a modifier identifying *Mr. and Mrs. Graf* in the sixth sentence.

Instead of the rough, scattered effect of the original, we now have two carefully organized sentences that lighten the reader's burden.

Check your sentence style now and then by looking at how your sentences begin. If too many of them begin with a subject-verb construction, you need to work on them. Look at the letter to Murray Klein on page 43. Eleven sentences comprise that letter. Here is how each begins: (1) subject-verb, (2) prepositional phrase, (3) subject-verb, (4) subordinate clause, (5) prepositional phrase, (6) subject-verb, (7) subordinate clause, (8) subject-verb, (9) verb, (10) subject-verb, (11) adverb. The variety of sentence styles in this letter will help keep Klein alert to Robin's message.

The following paragraph is dull and boring. Can you fix it?

(1) We ran Lyndon City's preservation project on a very low budget. (2) Two clerical assistants and I worked out of offices provided by the city. (3) We mailed letters to thousands of residents. (4) We planned and coordinated promotional parties and information sessions. (5) We developed grant proposals to federal and state agencies.

It could look like this:

(1) We ran Lyndon City's preservation project on a very low budget, working out of offices provided by the city. (2) With two clerical assistants, I mailed letters to thousands of residents, planned and coordinated promotional parties and information sessions, and developed grant proposals to federal and state agencies.

If an Idea is Important,
Give It a Sentence of Its Own

In the attempt to avoid Dick and Jane sentences, many business writers link up their sentences with conjunctions like *and, but,* or *so*:

> Enclosed is a copy of the bill I paid under protest, *and* I intend to contact the Consumer Protection Bureau of Texas within two weeks if the sum of $75.87 is not reimbursed me.

The effect, however, is clumsy. Compound constructions like this one add weight to the sentence while detracting from the importance of the individual ideas. Robin wants to give the reader some time to digest the fact that she did not pay the bill willingly. Similarly, she wants to stress that she will act quickly if the reader does not respond favorably. Her demand gains power when the ideas are isolated:

> Enclosed is a copy of the bill I paid under protest. I intend to contact the Consumer Protection Bureau of Texas within two weeks if the sum of $75.87 is not reimbursed me.

Here is another awkward compound construction:

> Our campaign was successful, *and* today Lyndon City's Sullivan landmark, old City Hall, is being renovated into office space for the business community.

When each sentence stands alone, the argument gathers strength:

> Our campaign was successful. Today Lyndon City's Sullivan landmark, old City Hall, is being renovated into office space for the business community.

When you want your readers to linger over an idea and thoroughly absorb its significance, put it in a sentence of its own. Each of the ideas in the following sentences gains intensity when allowed to stand alone:

Original:

- As one of the bright stars of our city, it has been attracting tourists for years and will attract more in years to come, *so* it is a structure we can truly be proud of.

Improved:

- As one of the bright stars of our city, it has been attracting tourists for years and will attract more in years to come. It is a structure we can truly be proud of.

Original:

- We also need to save our energy and natural resources *because* our economy today can't afford the wasteful consumption of the past.

Improved:

- We also need to save our energy and natural resources. Our economy today can't afford the wasteful consumption of the past.

Original:

- Please let us know how we should handle your order, for we want you to enjoy the best holiday season ever.

Improved:

- Please let us know how we should handle your order. We want you to enjoy the best holiday season ever.

When you want to lend equal weight to two or more ideas, often it is best not to put one of them into a subordinate clause. Consider the following example:

Even though I thought the charge was unfair, on January 20, under protest, I paid a bill for $1,218.37 to the Receiver of Taxes in Lyndon City, $75.87 of which represents a fine for late payment.

This sentence is smooth and grammatically correct. Yet how much more dramatically the ideas can be presented is shown in this revision:

On January 20, under protest, I paid a bill for $1,218.37 to the Receiver of Taxes in Lyndon City, $75.87 of which represents a fine for late payment. This charge is unfair.

In the earlier version Robin subordinated the *unfair charge* state-ment to the fact that she paid the bill, thereby making light of the idea. By lifting the imbedded idea and placing it in its own sentence, Robin calls attention to it and asserts her authority.

Dramatically calling attention to your ideas often requires no more than this simple technique of giving an idea its own sentence. Consider this sentence:

> The Preservation Committee has received a pledge of $2,000 from Mayor Brogan, $1,000 from Sidney Larson, and $1,000 each from the members of the Preservation Committee.

To draw more attention to the generosity of the key figures in the campaign and stimulate the reader's philanthropy, break the sentence down:

> Mayor Brogan has personally pledged $2,000 to the preservation campaign. Sidney Larson has sent his check for $1,000. Each of us on the Preservation Committee has pledged $1,000.

Better still, make each contribution stand out by allotting it its own paragraph.*

Keep the Parts of Your Sentence in the Right Order

The order in which you place words in a sentence is important to how quickly the sentence is understood. Can you understand this sen-tence?

> This historical landmark may be destroyed without your help.

If you can't understand it, it's because the writer has misplaced the phrase *without your help*. The sentence seems to say: *Even though you don't help us, the landmark will be destroyed.* In other words, it sounds as though the writer might *want* the landmark destroyed. The meaning changes when we shift the phrase to the beginning of the sentence:

> Without your help this historical landmark may be destroyed.

*See p. 141 under **The Paragraph**.

Now it is clear that the writer wants your help so that the landmark *won't* be destroyed.

Watch where you place qualifying phrases and clauses. The farther you place words from what they modify, the harder it will be to understand the sentence. The following sentences are all misleading because the words in italics are too far removed from the nouns they modify.

Original:
- To further maximize profits *on a daily basis* I monitored and balanced the bookstore stock personally.
  Problem:
- Profits were not maximized every day; the *books* were monitored daily.
  Improved:
- To further maximize profits, I monitored and balanced the bookstore stock personally on a daily basis.
  Original:
- I trained over 20 service and stock clerks, most of them students *in a three-year period.*
  Problem:
- The clerks were not students for three years; the writer trained them over a three-year period.
  Improved:
- In a three-year period I trained over 20 service and stock clerks, most of them students.
  Original:
- We ran Lyndon City's preservation project working out of offices provided by the city *on a very low budget.*
  Problem:
- The project, not the city offices, was run on a low budget.
  Improved:
- We ran Lyndon City's preservation project on a very low budget, working out of offices provided by the city.
  Original:
- I am urging you to support the bottle bill that will come before the Senate next month *as a voter in your district.*
  Problem:
- The bottle bill cannot be transformed into a voter.

Improved:

- As a voter in your district, I am urging you to support the bottle bill that will come before the Senate next month.

Original:

- Until 1957 Sullivan's gift was the seat of our local government, *when Lyndon City ran out of funds to modernize the interior and construct a more efficient airconditioning system.*

Problem:

- Lyndon City ran out of funds in 1957; get these facts together!

Improved:

- Sullivan's gift was the seat of our local government until 1957, when Lyndon City ran out of funds to modernize the interior and construct a more efficient airconditioning system.

When a sentence doesn't sound quite right, try to identify the misplaced words. Then lift them out of the sentence and put them next to the word(s) they modify.

Don't Dangle Your Modifiers

Closely related to defective word order is the modifier that dangles at the beginning of a sentence. Here is a sentence with a dangling modifier:

> *While walking to the computer room,* my BASIC manual fell to the floor.

The idea conveyed by this sentence is impossible. Computer manuals can fall to the floor but they're incapable of walking.

A dangling construction is one that has nothing to modify or that appears to modify a word it can't logically modify. *While walking to the computer room* dangles because we never learn from the sentence *who* was walking. When you start a sentence with a group of words that describes or implies an action, the reader expects to learn right away who or what is doing the action. Since *BASIC manual* is closest to the modifier we assume *it* to be the doer of the action. Because it's not, we have to revise the sentence to:

> While walking to the computer room, *I* dropped my BASIC manual on the floor.   *or*

> While *I* was walking to the computer room, my BASIC manual fell to the floor.

In the first revision we've changed the subject of the sentence to *I* so that the doer of the previously described action immediately follows the modifier. Now the opening phrase no longer hovers uncertainly over the rest of the sentence. The reader is told *who* was walking to the computer room.

In the second revision we've identified the person doing the walking in the modifier itself, changing the modifying phrase into a clause.* The rest of the sentence can then remain intact.

Make sure your modifying phrases don't hang too loosely from the rest of the sentence. Your readers shouldn't have to interrupt their reading to figure out what you mean. Study the next sentence:

At the age of eight, John's father married for the second time.

John's father, at age eight, is too young to marry even for the first time. It's not possible that *at the age of eight* can refer to John's or anyone else's father. To remedy this problem, identify exactly *who* was eight years old when John's father married again:

When John was eight, his father married for the second time.

In the following bewildering sentence, a contact lens suffers from an eye problem:

Having astigmatism, the traditional soft lens doesn't fit my needs.

The sentence must be revised to be valid:

Having astigmatism, *I find* the traditional soft lens doesn't fit my needs.

or

Because I have astigmatism, the traditional soft lens doesn't fit my needs.

In other words, establish a logical connection between your modifying phrase and the rest of the sentence. Here are two more examples:

*A clause is a group of words that contains a subject and a predicate.

Wrong:

- As one of the bright stars of our city, tourists have been and will continue to be attracted to it for years to come.
  Right:
- As one of the bright stars of our city, the *Sullivan Building* has been attracting tourists for years and will attract more in years to come.

or

Because the Sullivan Building is one of the bright stars of our city, tourists have been and will continue to be attracted to it for years to come.

Wrong:

- *Although arriving too late for a December 25 delivery,* I am assured the books will be here in time for delivery by January 1.
  Right:
- Although arriving too late for a December 25 delivery, *the books* will be here in time for delivery by January 1.

or

Although the books will arrive too late for a December 25 delivery, I am assured they'll be here in time for delivery by January 1.

Set Up Sequences
of Ideas in Parallel Form

To create a good visual image and help your reader move quickly from one idea to the next, your sentences must possess good parallel structure. Parallel structure means that pairs and sequences of ideas that are equally stressed are in the same grammatical form. Whenever you place two or more facts, ideas, or actions side by side in a sentence, make those facts look alike.

For example, in the following sentence, the bottle law has achieved three results:

Oregon's bottle law *has saved* taxpayers' money, *conserved* energy, and *created* jobs.

The italicized words, because they are all verbs in the past tense, are grammatically alike. Compare that sentence to this one:

Oregon's bottle law *has saved* taxpayers' money, *conserves* energy, and *creates* jobs.

The logic of the sentence is upset because the writer sets up an expectation in the reader's mind that isn't fulfilled. The first verb— *has saved*—sets the framework for the action in the sentence. Because the sentence starts this way, readers expect to be enlightened on what Oregon's bottle law has *already* achieved; they are thrown off balance when they stumble onto the present-tense verbs *conserves* and *creates*. The sentence suffers, therefore, from a lack of parallel structure.

Perhaps the best way to evaluate parallel structure is to study the headings of Robin's functional resume. Good parallel construction, by the way, is important when you design headings and subheadings in resumes and reports. These were Robin's resume headings:

- Sales and Fundraising Experience
- Administrative Ability
- Research and Writing Skills
- Work History
- Education

When you look closely at these headings, you'll notice that each one is composed of a noun and, with the exception of *Education*, one or more qualifying words preceding the noun. The first four, because of their almost identical grammatical form, are parallel. If the fifth section had been labeled *Educational Background*, it would have paralleled the other four more closely. In the interests of space Robin shortened it to *Education*. Not too much has been lost, however. When scanning the headings, the reader still gets a good overview of the resume contents without much interruption in thought.

The desire to prevent interruption of a chain of thought is the motive behind good parallel structure. The following set of headings temporarily disables the reader:

- Sales and Fundraising Experience
- Administration
- Research and Writing Engaged In

- History of Employment
- Schools Attended

Sales and Fundraising Experience gets the group off to a promising start, but the next four constructions divert the reader's attention. Readers' minds will wander when they light on *Administration*. Administration of *what*, or *what* administration, they might ask. The next construction—*Research and Writing Engaged In*—disorients readers further because, with the added verb, it isn't patterned after either of the first two headings. *History of Employment* is yet a different formation of words to deal with. (*Employment History* would at least have paralleled *Sales and Fundraising Experience*.) *Schools Attended*, while paralleling *Research and Writing Engaged In*, doesn't conform to the pattern of the others.

In other words, the writer's signals are not consistent. As a consequence, the reader is not tuned in to the writer's thought patterns and can't see at one quick glance the relationships among those headings on the page. It's a fact that the human mind sees relationships among ideas more quickly when the method of presenting those ideas reflects their relationship.

Let's look at another example of faulty parallelism from a resume, this time in a sentence.* Suppose, as an employer, you read this:

> Assignments included marketing research, analyzing the media, news releases, advertising copy, salesperson, bookkeeper, and I handled payroll.

This inconsistent method of describing duties is designed to confuse the reader. The first two items in the series (*marketing research* and *analyzing the media*) refer to activities, the next two (*news releases* and *advertising copy*) represent the products of activities; the following two (*salesperson* and *bookkeeper*) are job titles; and the last (*I handled payroll*) is a full sentence describing an activity. This sequence of facts needs to be reshaped into a coherent unit.

Follow the lead of the first two constructions and make the others parallel to them:

*Lack of parallel structure is especially damaging on a resume, where you should be doing your best to make your presentation reflect a coherent, logical mind.

Assignments included marketing research, media analysis,* news and copy writing, selling, bookkeeping, and payroll preparation.

If you prefer to talk about products rather than activities, transform the sequence to this:

Assignments included news releases, advertising copy, market research and media reports, sales, bank reconciliations, general ledger work, and payroll distribution.

So far we've been talking about fairly long sequences of facts. Yet faulty parallelism also arises when *two* ideas or activities are presented unequally, as in the following sentence:

Since several applicants for the position have strong qualifications in *accounting* as well as *being trained in customer service*, we are choosing the assistant manager from among them.

This sentence states that certain applicants are well qualified in *two* skills. Right? Yet one of the skills is described in a noun, the other in a verbal construction. More economical and simpler to grasp is this transformation into parallel language:

Since several applicants for the position have strong qualifications in *accounting* as well as *customer service*, we are choosing the assistant manager from among them.

Study these additional examples of faultily paired activities:

Faulty Sentence:
- Therefore I will appreciate your *looking into* the problem, Mr. Klein, and *to ask* the proper agency to return that amount to me.

Parallel Sentence:
- Therefore I will appreciate your *looking into* the problem, Mr. Klein, and *asking* the proper agency to return that amount to me.

Media analysis is preferable to *analyzing the media* because it more closely parallels *marketing research*. It's also shorter.

Faulty Sentence:

- When the new City Hall opened for business, the Sullivan building *was converted* to a commercial office building and *some small businesses rented the space.*

Parallel Sentence:

- When the new City Hall opened for business, the Sullivan building *was converted* to a commercial office building and *leased* to a number of small businesses.

Faulty parallelism also occurs in groups of three:

- I *mailed* letters to thousands of residents, *plan and coordinate* promotional parties and information sessions, and *developed* grant proposals. (Change the second activity to *planned and coordinated.*)
- Nine states have adopted a law that encourages people to take their cans and bottles back to the store instead of to *parking lots*, *highways*, and *littering the public parks*. (The last object of the preposition *to* should be *public parks.*)
- Nothing is more *unsanitary, dangerous,* and *it is also wasteful,* than a littered landscape. (*It is also wasteful* should be converted to *wasteful* to parallel the two adjectives.)
- I believe my ability to promote healthy relationships with *customers, vendors,* and *effectively communicating with employees* will go a long way toward making William McKinley's bookstore noticed throughout New York State. (Transform the last construction to *employees* to parallel *customers* and *vendors.*)

Make Your Numbers Visible

To aid the readability of your letter, use the journalist's rule of ten: Spell out all numbers ten and under; use figures for any number over ten:

six gallons	*Ten Easy Steps to Decorating Your Home*
16 years	19th-century buildings
100 copies	sixth century
12 gift cards	60 percent
600,000 tons	eight percent

Exception to this rule: When a number begins a sentence, always spell it out:

> *Eighty-five* years ago Sullivan's steel frame and vertical lines contrasted with the classic Greek and Roman styles of his contemporaries.

When writing dates, use the cardinal (1, 2, 3, etc.), not the ordinal (1st, 2nd, 3rd, etc.), number:

> May 22, 1985
> January 1
> the April 17 *Lyndon City Courier Express*

When writing dollar amounts, always use figures for amounts under $1 million:

> $1.15
> $65
> $200,000
> $123,111.55

For greater visibility, dollar amounts of $1 million and over may be typed this way:

> $7 million
> $1.1 million
> $650 billion

Only on checks and in legal documents, not in business letters, should a number be stated in both figures and words, as in:

> The borrower paid back two thousand dollars ($2,000) of the loan.

Underline to Emphasize Ideas

I have stressed that business letters are most effective when written in a conversational style. In keeping with this conversational style is the practice of underlining words that would be stressed if the sentence were spoken aloud, as in, for example:

> Although arriving too late for a December 25 delivery, the books <u>will</u> be here in time for delivery by January 1.*

Although this technique is appropriate in any business letter, it should not be overused. A letter in which every paragraph contains underlined words is too distracting to your reader. The underline key on your typewriter, however, does supply you with yet another strategy to gain emphasis for your ideas, and you should consider using it occasionally when your rhetorical intent is to demand or persuade.

The City Hall preservation letter (Model No. 7), for example, contains a sprinkling of underlined words that complements Robin's attempt to captivate her audience. Robin lends dramatic emphasis to her ideas by asking the reader to accent the word when reading the sentence:

- It has been proclaimed one of the ten most important buildings in the United States because it represents a truly <u>American</u> architecture.
- <u>We</u> have something <u>unique</u> in our city.
- Mr. Larson has expressed interest in moving here to coordinate the activities of the new museum, which would be the <u>first</u> architectural museum in the United States.
- Maybe "you can't fight City Hall," as they say. But the time has come to fight <u>for</u> it!

Used sparingly, the practice of underlining words for dramatic effect can help stimulate action on the part of your reader.

Don't Interrupt
Sentence Flow by Awkward Word Division

To keep your reader with you, avoid dividing words at the end of a line. Only when it would leave a huge gap at the end of a line and

---

*In addition to underlining for emphasis, remember that titles of books (*Four Seasons Gourmet Cookbook*), magazines (*Time, Fortune*), and newspapers (*Lyndon City Courier Express*) should be underlined in business letters.

weaken your right margin should you divide a word and carry it over to the next line. When you need to divide a word, use your dictionary to find out what its syllables are and divide only at a syllable break. In addition, follow these three simple rules:

1. Don't divide one-syllable words.
2. Don't leave fewer than three letters of a word at the end or beginning of a line.
3. Don't divide abbreviations or contractions.

THE PARAGRAPH

Shun Long Paragraphs

Unlike some fictional prose, business letters depend on short paragraphs to stimulate and sustain interest. Unless your letter contains only one or two sentences, never write a one-paragraph letter. Look at this letter:

> Dear Sir/Madam:
>
> Please reserve a double room for me and my husband for the nights of January 6 and 7. We will be arriving in New York on the morning of January 6 to attend a convention of the National Booksellers Association, which has recommended your hotel. We would appreciate a room on one of the top floors overlooking the park, to be charged to my VISA Account No. 0999 280 672 894. Please confirm in writing that you're holding the room.
>
> Sincerely,

Lumping all your sentences together creates poor visibility. Readers need some white space to rest their eyes and to encourage them to go on. White space is especially important in very long letters. Most people flip through the pages of a long letter before they begin to read it. If they see page after page of prose unrelieved by paragraph breaks, they may be discouraged from reading the letter. If they do begin to read it, they may soon find themselves wanting to take a nap. You do not want this to happen to *your* reader.

Look at the City Hall preservation letter (Model No. 7), and notice how Robin has set up the paragraphs to create plenty of white space. No paragraph is over six lines; some paragraphs are only one or two lines long. This arrangement is ideal for a letter longer than three pages.

Don't concentrate on paragraph structure when writing your first draft. Although much has been written about how every paragraph should have a topic sentence, don't concern yourself with the logistics of creating a paragraph. Some paragraph breaks will occur naturally to you; you won't even have to think about them. If they don't, just get your sentences down in the right order and break them into paragraphs when you revise.

Here is an example of how to do it. Assume the following is written as one paragraph in your first draft:

> I was chair of the committee formed to avert this disaster and preserve the work of one of our greatest American architects. Our campaign was successful. Today Lyndon City's Sullivan landmark, old City Hall, is being renovated into office space for the business community. This brings me to the purpose of my letter. In the fall my husband and I are returning to Western New York State. I am very interested in conducting your campaign to restore Buffalo's Hancock Building and would like to be considered for the job.

Ask yourself: Where is there a shift in ideas? *The answer is:* After the third sentence, where the writer stops talking about the Texas building and launches into the purpose of the letter. This spot, therefore, is the logical place to break up the paragraph.

If you can't readily identify where shifts in ideas occur, see if you can detect movements from general to specific or from specific to general. For example, consider the following paragraph:

> We ran Lyndon City's preservation project on a very low budget, working out of offices provided by the city. With two clerical assistants, I mailed letters to thousands of residents, planned and coordinated promotional parties and information sessions, and developed grant proposals to federal and state agencies. My knowledge of Sullivan's work, my established contacts with architects and historians interested in the preservation of 19th-century buildings, and my familiarity with Buffalo (having been born and raised there) will all, I feel, contribute toward the success of your efforts to preserve the Hancock Building.

The first two sentences discuss specific work Robin did on the Texas preservation project. The third sentence, on the other hand, generalizes the Texas work (her knowledge of Sullivan's work and her contacts both grew out of the Texas experience), and presents an additional qualification. Therefore, because the first two sentences describe specific work and the last sums up her general qualifications for the job, she should start a new paragraph with the third sentence.

Here is another example of a paragraph that's too long. See if you can decide where the natural breaks occur.

> What has happened to old City Hall since 1897? Sullivan's gift was the seat of our local government until 1957, when Lyndon City ran out of funds to modernize the interior and construct a more efficient airconditioning system. When the new City Hall opened for business, the Sullivan building was converted to a commercial office building and leased to a number of small businesses. It survived in this way until 1977, when a small fire in one of the offices frightened city officials into closing it to occupancy. Since then the city has been looking for a developer who will restore this masterwork as faithfully as possible to its original character and convert it into a high-quality office building.

As you will probably agree, beginning a new paragraph with the second sentence is logical. Questions followed by answers always signal a shift in idea. The fact that the second, third, fourth, and fifth sentences of the paragraph, which are all part of the answer, follow a chronological pattern indicates that each of them can be isolated in time. Therefore, the paragraph could be broken up at any point in this sequence of ideas. Make a judgment about where the break would *look* best. Starting a new paragraph with the fourth sentence is a good choice because the last two paragraphs are then spatially balanced:

> What has happened to old City Hall since 1897?
>
> Sullivan's gift was the seat of our local government until 1957, when Lyndon City ran out of funds to modernize the interior and construct a more efficient airconditioning system. When the new City Hall opened for business, the Sullivan building was converted to a commercial office building and leased to a number of small businesses.

It survived in this way until 1977, when a small fire in one of the offices frightened city officials into closing it to occupancy. Since then the city has been looking for a developer who will restore this masterwork as faithfully as possible to its original character and convert it into a high-quality office building.

Your decisions on paragraph structure should be ultimately based on common sense.

Consider the One-Sentence Paragraph

Just as thoughts gain intensity when they appear in sentences of their own, these thoughts will attract even more attention when surrounded by white space. Near the end of the City Hall preservation letter (Model No. 7), Robin wishes the reader to recognize the sacrifices that other people have made to save the Sullivan landmark. To slow the reader down so that each idea will sink in independently of the others, she states each idea in a separate paragraph:

Mayor Brogan has personally pledged $2,000 to the preservation campaign.

Sidney Larson has sent his check for $1,000.

Each of us on the Preservation Committee has pledged $1,000.

If you want to startle the eye, emphasize your idea, and imprint it on the reader's memory, consider using the one-sentence paragraph. The pause you create will encourage your reader to fully digest the idea before moving on.

Obviously this is a technique that should not be overworked. In one-page letters it should be used sparingly. In long letters that seek to evoke a reaction, however, it can be an effective way to stimulate reader interest. The City Hall preservation letter, for example, contains 34 paragraphs, 21 of which are one-sentence paragraphs.

The letter to Senator Sedita (Model No. 8), another persuasive letter, employs this strategy effectively to grab the reader's attention at the start. Compare the following opener with the three-paragraph structure seen on page 74:

Last week three children were hurt at the Lambert Street school when they stumbled on broken glass scattered on the playground. A Lyndon County farmer punctured two tractor tires last month when he ran over a broken beer bottle on Route 59. In the meantime, the Sterling Street landfill has been running over with empty bottles and cans.

Allotting each sentence its own paragraph heightens the intensity of each and makes a more lasting impression on the reader.

List Ideas Vertically to Create White Space

Another way of making your points more visually attractive and durable is by setting them up in vertical lists rather than stringing them horizontally into a paragraph. The third paragraph of the letter to Global Vision (Model No. 1) could have been constructed this way:

I will be thankful for any information you can send. In addition, I would like answers to the following questions: (1) Can they be worn during the night; i.e., are they designed for extended wear? (2) What has been the success rate for wearers so far? (3) What is the price to the consumer? (4) Has a bifocal been designed for this type of lens? (5) Where are the lenses being distributed? Is there a distributor in my area?

As you can see, no one question stands out from the rest. When they are listed vertically and separated from each other by a double space, however, the individual questions gain prominence, and your chances for getting each of them answered increases. Your readers will not have to fish through a paragraph for the points they need to address.

Because you want your reader relaxed and able to decipher your message easily, whenever possible organize your points into vertical lists. Vertical lists are especially important in a resume. Be willing to sacrifice some space to make your outstanding accomplishments and activities leap out at the reader. Compare the following section to the vertical arrangement of the same facts in Robin's functional resume (Model No. 11):

SALES AND FUNDRAISING EXPERIENCE:

Developed and ran promotional campaign as chair of preservation committee for Texas landmark, achieving goal of over $1 million; identified, implemented, and advertised new brand of bookstore merchandise, resulting in 25% increase in profit; established wage incentives for bookstore personnel, which increased total sales for two consecutive years; sold Avon products to over 400 clients, grossing $12,000 one year.

The preceding arrangement considerably weakens the impact of this survey of skills.

Link up Ideas with Transition Words

To help your readers and yourself see the relationships among your ideas, transition words are often useful. When we speak, we build on our thoughts by adding, contrasting, showing results, elaborating, and moving backward and forward in time. Within a paragraph or between paragraphs, we can show readers how our thoughts are moving by signaling with words like *in addition, however, therefore, meanwhile,* or *finally*. The italicized words in the following paragraphs signal such shifts in thought:

- As you know, nine states have adopted a law that encourages people to take their cans and bottles back to the store instead of to parking lots, highways, and public parks. *Furthermore*, these regulations have lightened America's landfills, which are fast running out of space.

- We were eagerly awaiting the arrival of this publication after its favorable review in Publishers Weekly. *In fact*, several of our regular customers have already requested the book. You can imagine our disappointment, *therefore*, when we opened the shipment to find a large faded spot across the upper lefthand corner of each of the covers.

- Age alone does not determine a landmark's value. The White House and Mount Vernon, *for example*, are older buildings that impress us with a sense of history. Next to our own Sullivan building, *however*, they are not architectural masterpieces.

Place the following words between clauses and sentences to connect your ideas:

To connect parallel ideas:	also, furthermore, in addition, similarly
To connect contrasting ideas:	but, yet, however, on the contrary, nevertheless, on the other hand
To connect cause and effect:	therefore, as a result, thus, so, consequently
To connect two ideas in time:	meanwhile, at the same time
To introduce an example:	for example, for instance
To introduce an elaboration:	in fact, specifically, most important
To introduce a backward movement in time:	before that, previously, earlier, formerly
To introduce a forward movement in time:	next, then, subsequently, eventually, finally

Transition words, of course, will not show a logical progression of thought when there is none to begin with; so don't rely on them to make your ideas coherent. Yet when a logical sequence of ideas already exists, transition words will allow your reader to glide more easily from one idea to the next.

MODERN BUSINESS STYLE

Abandon Business Cliches

Many years ago when business letters were highly formal and impersonal, certain expressions became standardized as part of every business writer's vocabulary. Phrases like *at your earliest convenience* and *under separate cover* were to be found in almost every business communication. These expressions, today referred to as business cliches or *rubber stamps*, have become so worn out with the passage of time they have lost their functional value. Unfortunately, people with a fragmented knowledge of business letter style sometimes believe that mastering a few of these business cliches will help them to construct an acceptable business letter. This belief is wrong.

Far from making a business letter acceptable, the use of standard, made-to-measure phrases in a contemporary business communication deadens your prose and dilutes your message. Imagine that Robin had begun her letter (Model No. 10) to Shelley Sebouhian this way:

> *Enclosed herewith please find* my resume *as per* your announcement in last week's <u>Chronicle of Higher Education</u>.

Or that she chose to open a letter to a customer like this:

> *Please be advised that* your order is greatly appreciated.

Something is lost in this transformation into business jargon. No longer is the style friendly and conversational. Instead, the message is dulled by words that serve no purpose.

Here are some business cliches you should make every effort to avoid:

Cliche	*Alternative*
Please find enclosed herewith . . . (or any variations of this theme)	Enclosed is . . . *or* Here is . . .
In accordance with your request . . . As per your request . . .	As you requested, . . .
I wish to acknowledge receipt of . . .	I have received . . .
Please be advised that . . .	Strike it out and begin with the next word.
It has come to my attention that . . .	Strike it out and think of a better way to begin.
under separate cover	separately
at your earliest convenience	soon, as soon as you can

Eliminate these stale expressions (and others like them) from your vocabulary, and I guarantee you will almost immediately begin to write more interesting, thoughtful business letters.

Make a special effort to censor cliches from your closing remarks and you will be well on your way to becoming a professional communicator. Here are the most common rubber stamp closings:

- Thank you for your time and cooperation.

- Thank you in advance for your assistance/attention in this matter.
- I will appreciate hearing from you at your earliest convenience.
- If I can be of any further assistance/If you have any further questions, please do not hesitate to call on me.

The model letters in this book show how to express appreciation for your reader's efforts by tailoring your remarks to the subject of the letter. Always close your letters with an individualized, personal approach to the subject. If you enlist one of the preceding cliches (or variations of them) to end your letter, you will depersonalize your message and diminish empathy.

Adopt Specific, Concrete Words

Another remnant of a bygone era that lingers on in some quarters is the use of abstract, legalistic words that draw attention to themselves rather than the idea expressed. Words like *in this matter, subject policy*, and *said date* are lazy words that fail to communicate concise information to the reader. A typical example of this overstuffed, legal-sounding prose is the following:

> *It has come to my attention* that *subject policy*, due on January 6 and *enclosed herein for your perusal*, will be renewed as of *said date*.

This sentence, although it contains four verbs, fails to portray any sense of action. When your sentences do not clarify activity, rarely will they motivate your readers to act upon them.

If you choose the vague, abstract word over the concrete, you communicate a lazy, inconsiderate attitude toward your reader. Here are some sentences that lack energy (the lazy phrases are in italics):

- I will appreciate your looking into *this matter*.
- It has been proclaimed one of the ten most important buildings in the United States because of *its many unusual aspects*.
- Let's all pull together *in this effort*.
- I have held several part-time and temporary positions in advertising and *related fields*.

- I developed, coordinated, and supervised *things* for a large bookstore operation.

Nouns that name qualities or concepts (such as *matter, thing, factor, aspect, area*), instead of specific persons, places, objects, and actions, create cloudy impressions instead of clear images.

Study the following corrupted version of paragraph five of Model No. 12:

My knowledge of *the field*, my contacts with *people*, and my familiarity with Buffalo will all, I feel, contribute to the success of your efforts *in this area*.

The shortage of specific, concrete words in that passage contrasts sharply to the tangible, descriptive language of this sentence from Model No. 7:

Eighty-five years ago Sullivan's steel frame and vertical lines contrasted with the classic Greek and Roman styles of his contemporaries.

Watch the Spelling
of These Commonly Confused Words

The clarity of your communication can be affected adversely by the misuse of certain words frequently used in business letters. The list below covers those words most commonly confused.

accept/except. *Accept* is a *verb* meaning "agree to take" or "receive as true." Examples:

- Since the book should prove to be a popular gift item, you can understand why we cannot *accept* this shipment.
- To move someone to *accept* your ideas, you sometimes have to create a whole new state of mind in your audience.

The word *except* is a preposition or conjunction that means "excluding" or "only." Examples:

- The bookstore manager accepted all the reports *except* John's.
- *Except* for the Burbane Building in Chicago, old City Hall is the only example of the early skyscraper still alive.

affect/effect.   Except for its special use as a noun in psychology, *affect* is a *verb* meaning "to influence":

- The beginning *affects* the readability of the entire letter.
- If you reflect uncertainty, your letter will *affect* the reader unfavorably and lessen your credibility.

Effect is the *noun* that means "result, outcome; the condition of being in full force." Examples:

- Sometimes personal contact has more *effect* than a letter.
- These local, human interest stories are specific *effects* of Texas' lack of a bottle regulation.

There is so much confusion over these words because *effect* can also be used as a verb. When it acts as a verb it means "to bring about" or "accomplish," as in:

- His lawyer *effected* a settlement.
- You write letters because you wish to make changes in your life, and you want these changes to be *effected* smoothly.

The difference between the verbs *affect* and *effect* is shown in the following sentences:

- Martin Luther King *affected* the civil rights movement.
- Martin Luther King *effected* a revolution in civil rights.

The first sentence says that King influenced (or had an *effect* on) the civil rights movement; the second sentence states that he brought about a revolution in civil rights *singlehandedly*.

assure/ensure/insure.   These three verbs have slight differences in meaning. The word *assure* means "to set a person's mind at ease"; the action of the verb is always toward *some person*. Examples:

- This thorough attention to detail *assures* Mrs. Washington her problem is in good hands.

- When you turn down job applicants, perhaps you can *assure* them that their qualifications are strong and their opportunities for employment elsewhere promising.

Ensure and *insure*, on the other hand, both mean "to make sure" or "to guarantee," but *insure* is used only in reference to insurance contracts. Examples:

- You will need to reexamine those words to *ensure* they are organized logically and presented clearly.
- When you want to *ensure* that your reader receives your message, it is worth the extra investment to send your letter certified mail.
- When you send a letter registered mail, you *insure* its contents against loss or theft.

capital/capitol. *Capitol*, a word with many meanings, serves the following functions:

1. As an adjective, it means "chief in importance":

- Center each line and type your name in *capital* letters.
- The bookstore manager made a *capital* blunder.

2. As a noun, *capital* means "wealth in the form of money or property":

- The bookstore lacked the *capital* to make the investment.

3. As a noun, it means "a city serving as a seat of government":

- Albany is the *capital* of New York State.

The word *capitol* refers only to the building(s) in which a legislative body meets:

- If the legislature is in session, send your letter to the *capitol* building (or simply the *capitol*).

cite/site/sight. *Cite* is the verb; *site*, the noun. To *cite* something is "to refer to or quote an authority," as in:

- The following example *cites* the facts your reader needs to identify your problem quickly.

The noun *site* means "a place or plot of land":

- This group plans to tear it down and build an apartment complex on the *site*.

Sight, on the other hand, means "the ability to see" or "something that is seen," as in *The Sullivan building is an impressive sight*. The fact that *sight* is also used as a verb meaning "to see" (as in *They sighted land*) is a cause for confusion. However, it is rarely used as a verb in business writing. When you are in a quandary over which word to use, let your dictionary set you straight!

complement/compliment. Watch these two. They can be tough to distinguish between because both can be used as nouns *or* verbs. The noun *compliment* means "honor or praise; a flattering remark," as in:

- Your professor paid you a *compliment*.

Used as a verb, it means "to show regard or respect for; to pay a *compliment* to":

- Your professor *complimented* you on your term project.

The adjective *complimentary*, therefore, is a word expressing praise. It also refers to something given free or as a favor. Examples:

- The <u>Lyndon City Courier Express</u> made a number of *complimentary* remarks about the Sullivan building.
- To make up for your loss, we are sending you a *complimentary* copy of Walter Hampton's <u>The Making of a City</u>.
- The last sentence of your message is followed by the *complimentary* close.

The noun *complement*, which derives from the word *complete*, although used infrequently, means "anything that completes a whole; a complete set":

- I can offer your organization a *complement* of education and experience.

Used more often as a verb, it means "to complete or make perfect":

- Robin expresses her desire to serve William McKinley State University, *complementing* the closing sentence of her opening paragraph.
- The letter contains a sprinkling of underlined words that *complements* Robin's attempt to captivate her audience.

Likewise, the adjective *complementary* refers to objects or ideas that *complete* something:

- I hope you feel my education and employment history are *complementary* to your needs.

compose/comprise. A common assumption in business and other professional writing is that these two words are interchangeable. The word *compose*, however, means "to form by putting together":

- Most of us can use some tips in *composing* a letter motivating citizens to contribute to a cause.
- A letter of persuasion *is composed of* three main parts.

The expression *is composed of* is correctly phrased in the preceding sentence. It is never correct, however, to write *is comprised of*. The word *comprise* is not identical to *compose*. *Comprise* means "to contain; to be made up of." Note well its use in the following sentences:

- When your closing *comprises* (never *is comprised of*) more than one word, capitalize only the first word.
- If your mailing list *comprises* (never *is comprised of*) hundreds of names, typing each letter by hand is a waste of humanpower and time.

- You should double space your message only in brief letters *comprising* two or three sentences.

Remember that the *whole* always *comprises* (contains) its *parts*. You cannot reverse a sentence to read: *Hundreds of names comprise the mailing list*. Rather, the mailing list (whole) comprises the names (parts).

council/counsel/consul.   *Council*, which is always a *noun*, refers to a group of people that acts as a governing body:

- In America any company, government, agency, *council*, committee, or other organization of people is considered a single unit.

Counsel can be used as either a noun *or* a verb. As a noun, it usually means "advice":

- He asked for my *counsel* regarding the Sullivan building.

It also refers to a lawyer (or group of lawyers) who handles court cases:
- I reviewed and edited radio, TV and print advertising for two major tobacco companies, working directly with corporation *counsel* and advertising managers.

The verb *counsel* means "to advise":

- He *counselled* them to move slowly in the case.

Consul, on the other hand, refers to an officer in the foreign service of a country:

- The U.S. *consul* to Great Britain reviewed the document.

dual/duel.   The word *duel*, a noun, should never be confused with the adjective *dual*. A *duel* refers to a combat between two people, as in "to fight a *duel*." *Dual* means "double; twofold":

- Only one side of your *dual* purpose should be revealed here— that of retaining your reader's good will.

eminent/imminent. The word *eminent* means "famous" or "prominent" and is often used to characterize people:

- Mayor Brogan and other *eminent* citizens of Lyndon City are supporting the campaign.

Another common use of the word is in the expression *eminent domain*, which refers to the right of a government to take over private property for public use.

Imminent means "about to happen":

- The passage of the bottle bill is *imminent*.

formally/formerly. The adverb *formally* means "in a ceremonious manner; according to convention":

- The job applicant was *formally* introduced to the committee, which made him uncomfortable.

Formerly, on the other hand, means "at a former (previous) time":

- Mr. and Mrs. Graf *formerly* owned the property.

personal/personnel. Confusion of these two will limit your credibility as a writer. *Personal* is the *adjective* meaning "private" or "pertaining to an individual person":

- Business letters today reflect a more *personal*, conversational style.
- If you feel you can handle the problem better through *personal* contact, do so.

Personnel is a *noun* that refers to a group of people employed by an organization:

- There is no standard operating procedure for the hiring of *personnel*.

- In some companies an applicant should contact the director of *personnel*.
- She is an individual who can cut costs, increase sales, and solve *personnel* problems.

In the last sentence, *personnel problems* means "employee problems," which may or may not be *personal* in nature.

Do not use the word *personnel* when speaking of specific members of a group:

Incorrect:
- Robin hired, trained, and supervised six *personnel*.
Correct:
- Robin hired, trained, and supervised six *people*.

principal/principle.   Try to remember that the word *principle* can only be a noun, while *principal* is either a noun *or* adjective. *Principle* has only one meaning; it refers to a rule or basic truth:

- Those who fail to appreciate this *principle* and start off a letter with *I regret to inform you that* . . . show no regard for the person at the other end.
- Robin is a person of strong *principles*.

Principal, on the other hand, has many meanings. As a noun, it can mean "a sum of money on which interest is paid":

- He pays *principal* and interest on his mortgage loan every month.

It also means "chief official" of a school or corporation:

- The *principal* of a high school is its busiest administrator.
- The *principals* of large organizations may be more interested than some of their employees in what customers or constituents are thinking.

Used as an adjective, *principal* means "primary; most important":

- The *principal* purpose of all business communication is to tell readers what they need to know to solve your problem.

- The *Million Dollar Directory* lists the size of the company, its most recent sales and income figures, and the *principal* officers.

Note that, in the last sentence, *principals* could be substituted for *principal officers* with no change in meaning.

   respectfully/respectively.   *Respectfully*, meaning "with respect," refers to a way to treat people and property:

- Treat your readers *respectfully* if you want your letters to bring results.

Formal minutes of meetings often end with *Respectfully submitted*. Although it is considered servile and fawning today, years ago people used to close correspondence with *Respectfully yours.**
   Respectively, however, has an entirely different meaning; it means "in the order designated," as in:

- The first and second awards in the writing contest went to Robin Redgrave and Leslie Esmerada *respectively*.

   stationary/stationery.   *Stationery* is the noun referring to writing paper and envelopes. *Stationary* is the adjective meaning "fixed in position; not moving." Examples:

- *Stationery* with floral designs running through the page should not be used for business letters.
- The house trailer had remained *stationary* for five years.

Sprinkle Your Prose
with Contractions for the Right Rhythm

While you are editing your letters for precision and clarity, watch for opportunities to make your sentences smoother and user-friendly. A conversational style can often be enhanced by using contractions in place of full words. Note the differences in rhythm and level of formality of these sentences:

---

*According to contemporary American protocol, the only person to whom you should close a letter with *Respectfully yours* is the President of the United States. See first footnote to Appendix A.

Original Version:
- Because I have astigmatism, however, the traditional soft lens *does not* fit my needs.

Improved Version:
- Because I have astigmatism, however, the traditional soft lens *doesn't* fit my needs.

Original Version:
- Not included on my resume are a number of references I can send you after *you have* reviewed this application.

Improved Version:
- Not included on my resume are a number of references I can send you after *you've* reviewed this application.

Deciding when to contract words depends on the number and length of words in your sentence and where you want the stress to fall. Often a sentence with more than one verbal construction will begin to stumble if all the verbs are spelled out. Example:

- Since *we need* these books for our Christmas sales, *we are confident you will get* the duplicate order to us quickly.

The economy and cadence of the sentence are improved when the last verb is contracted:

- Since we need these books for our Christmas sales, we are confident *you'll get* the duplicate order to us quickly.

Don't Be Afraid
to Address Your Reader by Name

To lessen the distance between you and your reader and personalize your message further, consider working your reader's name into the body of the letter. People like to be addressed by name. Try it occasionally in a letter:

- Therefore I will appreciate your looking into the problem, *Mr. Klein*, and asking the proper agency to return that amount to me.
- Although arriving too late for a December 25 delivery, *Mrs. Washington*, the books will be here in time for delivery by January 1.

Do not overdo this technique, however. Once in a letter is enough. Frequent use of the reader's name will make you sound oversolicitous and phony.

Eliminate Sexist Words from Your Vocabulary

With increasing numbers of women in the work force, you must be sure no sexist overtones appear in your correspondence. The generic *he, his,* and *him* are not acceptable when speaking of individuals whose sex is not known. Unfortunately, our language has no third person singular pronoun that refers to both males and females. When faced with a pronoun problem, however, you have three options to choose from:

1. Eliminate the pronoun reference entirely.
2. Change all pronoun references to the plural.
3. Substitute *he or she (him/her, his/hers)* for the masculine pronoun.

When faced with an inappropriate masculine pronoun, first see if the word can be omitted without loss of meaning. In the following sentence the word *his* can be eliminated:

Sexist Reference:
- Each staff member has been hired on the basis of *his* education and experience.

Nonsexist Reference:
- Each staff member has been hired on the basis of education and experience.

If it would be awkward to strike out the pronoun, change the pronoun and its antecedents to the plural. Example:

Sexist Reference:
- The best way to keep *a customer* happy is to give *him his* money's worth.

Nonsexist Reference:
- The best way to keep *customers* happy is to give *them their* money's worth.

These two methods will usually work to eliminate gender-based discrimination. Occasionally, however, a situation arises in which it is not possible to use them, as in the following sentence:

The director of personnel will meet with the candidates in *his* office.

Assuming the sex of the personnel director is unknown and that only one director is being spoken of, we are forced to adopt the third alternative and write the sentence this way:

The director of personnel will meet with the candidates in *his or her* office.

The *he or she/his or her* construction should be used sparingly. Frequent use of double pronouns makes for awkward, cumbersome sentences. So whenever possible try to eliminate the pronoun altogether or substitute plural references.

Like the generic *he* constructions, *man* and *-man* words should be stricken from your business vocabulary. Here is a list of genderless words that are acceptable substitutes for old-style references to people and occupations:

Use:	*Not:*
assistant or secretary	gal Friday
businessperson	businessman
broker, go-between	middleman
chair or chairperson	chairman
firefighter	fireman
flight attendant	stewardess
homemaker	housewife
human beings	man
humanity, humankind	mankind
humanpower, labor force	manpower
layperson	layman
mail carrier	mailman
police officer	policeman
Representative, member of Congress	congressman
salesperson, sales rep	salesman
speaker, spokesperson	spokesman
stock clerk	stock boy
supervisor	foreman

RECOMMENDED FORMS OF ADDRESS FOR GOVERNMENT OFFICIALS AND OTHER PROFESSIONALS

Political Leaders—Federal Government

Addressee	Inside Address and Envelope	Salutation
The President	The President The White House Washington, DC 20500	Dear Mr. (Madam) President:*
Spouse of the President	Mrs. (Mr.) (full name) The White House Washington, DC 20500	Dear Mrs. (Mr.) (surname):
Assistant to the President	Honorable (full name) Assistant to the President The White House Washington, DC 20500	Dear Mr. (M's) (surname):
The Vice President	The Vice President United States Senate Washington, DC 20510	Dear Mr. (Madam) Vice President:
Cabinet members	Honorable (full name) Secretary of (department) Washington, DC (zip)	Dear Mr. (Madam) Secretary:
Attorney general	Honorable (full name) Attorney General Washington, DC (zip)	Dear Mr. (Madam) Attorney General:

*The conventional closing for a letter to the United States President is *Respectfully yours. Sincerely yours* is appropriate for all other officials.

Addressee	*Inside Address and Envelope*	*Salutation*
Assistant, Deputy, or Under Secretaries	Honorable (full name) Assistant (Deputy/Under) Secretary of (department) Washington, DC (zip)	Dear Mr. (M's) (surname):
Senator (Senate office address)	Honorable (full name) United States Senate Washington, DC 20510	Dear Senator (surname):
(hometown address)	Honorable (full name) United States Senator (local address)	Dear Senator (surname):
Representative (Congress office address)	Honorable (full name) House of Representatives Washington, DC 20515	Dear Mr. (M's) (surname):
(hometown address)	Honorable (full name) Representative in Congress (local address)	Dear Mr. (M's) (surname):
The Chief Justice	Chief Justice of the United States The Supreme Court Washington, DC 20543	Dear Mr. (Madam) Chief Justice:
Associate Justice	Mr. (Madam) Justice (surname) The Supreme Court Washington, DC 20543	Dear Mr. (Madam) Justice:
Judge of a court	Honorable (full name) Judge of the (name of court) (local address)	Dear Judge (surname):
Clerk of a court	Mr. (M's) (full name) Clerk of the (name of court) (local address)	Dear Mr. (M's) (surname):
Head of federal office or agency (example)	Honorable (full name) Comptroller General of the United States General Accounting Office Washington, DC 20548	Dear Mr. (M's) (surname):
Head of federal commission	Honorable (full name) Chairperson, (name of commission) Washington, DC (zip)	Dear Mr. (Madam) Chairperson:

Addressee	*Inside Address and Envelope*	*Salutation*
American Ambassador	Honorable (full name) American Ambassador (city, country)	Dear Mr. (Madam) Ambassador:
American Consul General	Mr. (M's) (full name) American Consul General (city, country)	Dear Mr. (M's) (surname):
Ambassador to the United States	His (Her) Excellency (full name) Ambassador of (country) (U.S. address)	Dear Mr. (Madam) Ambassador:

Political Leaders—State and Local Government

Governor	Honorable (full name) Governor of (state) (city, state, zip)	Dear Governor (surname):
Lieutenant Governor	Honorable (full name) Lieutenant Governor of (state) (city, state, zip)	Dear Mr. (M's) (surname):
Secretary of State	Honorable (full name) Secretary of State of (state) (city, state, zip)	Dear Mr. (Madam) Secretary:
State attorney general	Honorable (full name) Attorney General State of (state) (city, state, zip)	Dear Mr. (Madam) Attorney General:
Chief justice of a state supreme court	Honorable (full name) Chief Justice Supreme Court of the State of (state name) (city, state, zip)	Dear Mr. (Madam) Chief Justice:
Judge	Honorable (full name) (name of court) (city, state, zip)	Dear Judge (surname):
State auditor, comptroller or treasurer	Honorable (full name) State Auditor (Comptroller/ Treasurer) State of (state) (city, state, zip)	Dear Mr. (M's) (surname):

Addressee	*Inside Address and Envelope*	*Salutation*
State senator	Honorable (full name) (name, of state) Senate (city, state, zip)	Dear Senator (surname):
State representative, assembly member, or delegate	Honorable (full name) (name of state) House of Representatives (Assembly/ House of Delegates) (city, state, zip)	Dear Mr. (M's) (surname):
Mayor	Honorable (full name) Mayor of (city) (city, state, zip)	Dear Mayor (surname):

Religious Leaders

The pope	His Holiness Pope (religious name) State of Vatican City Italy	Most Holy Father:
Catholic cardinal	His Eminence (first name) Cardinal (surname) Archbishop of (diocese) (city, state, zip)	Dear Cardinal (surname):
Catholic archbishop or bishop	The Most Reverend (full name) Archbishop (Bishop) of (diocese) (city, state, zip)	Dear Archbishop (Bishop) (surname):
Catholic Monsignor	The Right Reverend Monsignor (full name) (city, state, zip)	Dear Monsignor (surname):
Catholic priest	The Reverend (full name) (name of church or institution) (street address) (city, state, zip)	Dear Father (surname):
Mother Superior	Mother (religious name) (surname) (title, name of institution) (street address) (city, state, zip)	Dear Mother (religious name):
Nun	Sister (religious name)	Dear Sister (religious name):

Addressee	*Inside Address and Envelope*	*Salutation*
	or	
	Sister (first name and (surname) (name of institution) (street address) (city, state, zip)	Dear Sister (first name):
Rabbi	Rabbi (full name) (name of synagogue or institution) (street address) (city, state, zip)	Dear Rabbi (surname):
Protestant bishop	The Right Reverend (full name) Bishop of (city) (city, state, zip)	Dear Bishop (surname):
Protestant Dean	The Very Reverend (full name) Dean of (name of church) (street address) (city, state, zip)	Dear Dean (surname):
Protestant minister	The Reverend (full name) (name of church or institution) (street address) (city, state, zip)	Dear Reverend (surname):
Chaplain	Chaplain (full name) (rank, branch of service) (post office address)	Dear Chaplain (surname):

College and University Leaders

College or university president (with doctorate)	Dr. (full name), President (name of institution) (street address) (city, state, zip)	Dear Dr. (surname):
(without doctorate)	Mr. (M's) (full name), President	Dear Mr. (M's) (surname):

Addressee	Inside Address and Envelope	Salutation
College or university vice president (with doctorate)*	Dr. (full name), Vice President of (division) (name of institution)	Dear Dr. (surname):
Dean (with doctorate)*	Dr. (full name), Dean (school or division) (name of institution)	Dear Dean (surname):
Professor	Professor (full name) Department of (name) (name of institution)	Dear Professor (surname):

Other Professionals

Addressee	Inside Address and Envelope	Salutation
Physician	(full name), M.D. (street address) (city, state, zip)	Dear Dr. (surname):
Lawyer	Mr. (M's) (full name) Attorney at Law (law firm name) (street address) (city, state, zip)	Dear Mr. (M's) (surname):
Military officer	(rank and full name, branch of service) (division) (post office address)	Dear (rank and surname):

*For officials without the doctorate, follow the format for college or university president.

COMMON BUSINESS ABBREVIATIONS

Abbreviations followed by an asterisk (*) can be used in inside addresses when there is a need to conserve space.

A.A.	Associate in Arts
A.A.S.	Associate in Applied Science
acct., a/c	account
ADP	automatic data processing
AEC	Atomic Energy Commission
AFL–CIO	American Federation of Labor and Congress of Industrial Organizations
a.k.a.	also known as
AMA	American Management Association; American Medical Association
AMEX	American Stock Exchange
amt.	amount
AP	Associated Press
APO*	Army Post Office
Apt.*	apartment
ASAP	as soon as possible
Assn.*	association
Asst.*	assistant
Attn.*	Attention
ATM	automated teller machine
atty.	attorney
Ave.*	Avenue

B.A. or A.B.	Bachelor of Arts
bal.	balance
BBB	Better Business Bureau
B.D.	Bachelor of Divinity
B/L	bill of lading
Bldg.*	Building
Blvd.*	Boulevard
Bros.*	Brothers
B.S.	Bachelor of Science
bu	bushel(s)
Capt.*	Captain
cc	carbon copy
CD	certificate of deposit
CEO	chief executive officer
CIA	Central Intelligence Agency
Cir.*	Circle
CLU	Chartered Life Underwriter
cm	centimeter
CO	Commanding officer
Co.*	Company
c/o	in care of
C.O.D.	cash on delivery
Comp.*	Comptroller
cont.	continued
Corp.*	Corporation
C.P.A.	Certified Public Accountant
CPI	Consumer Price Index
cr.	credit
CSC	Civil Service Commission
C.S.T.	central standard time
Ct.*	Court
D.A.	Doctor of Arts
d.b.a.	doing business as
D.D.	Doctor of Divinity
D.D.S.	Doctor of Dental Science (Surgery)
Dept.*	Department
Dir.*	Director
disc.	discount
Dist.*	District
Dist. Ct.*	District Court
Div.*	Division

dam	decameter
dm	decimeter
do.	ditto
DOT	Department of Transportation
doz.	dozen
DP	data processing
Dr.*	Drive; doctor; debit
D.S.T.	daylight saving time
D.V.M.	Doctor of Veterinary Medicine
E.*	East
ea.	each
Ed.D.	Doctor of Education
EDP	electronic data processing
E.D.T.	eastern daylight time
EEOC	Equal Employment Opportunity Commission
e.g.	for example
enc.	enclosure
e.o.m.	end of month
EPA	Environmental Protection Agency
Esq.*	Esquire
E.S.T.	eastern standard time
et al.	and others
etc.	and so forth
Expy.*	Expressway
FBI	Federal Bureau of Investigation
FCC	Federal Communications Commission
FDA	Food and Drug Administration
FDIC	Federal Deposit Insurance Corporation
Fed.*	Federal
ff.	and following pages
FHA	Federal Housing Administration
FICA	Federal Insurance Contributions Act
fig.	figure
FNMA	Federal National Mortgage Association (Fannie Mae)
F.O.B.	free on board
FPC	Federal Power Commission
FRS	Federal Reserve System
ft	foot, feet
FTC	Federal Trade Commission
fwd.	forward
FYI	for your information

gal	gallon
GAO	General Accounting Office
Gen.*	General
GNMA	Government National Mortgage Association (Ginnie Mae)
GNP	gross national product
Gov.	Governor
Govt.*	Government
GPO	Government Printing Office
HBR	Harvard Business Review
HEW	Department of Health, Education and Welfare
hm	hectometer
Hon.*	Honorable
HQ	headquarters
hr.	hour
Hts.*	Heights
HUD	Housing and Urban Development
Hwy. *	Highway
ICC	Interstate Commerce Commission
i.e.	that is
IMF	International Monetary Fund
in.	inch, inches
Inc.*	Incorporated
Ins.*	Insurance
Inst.*	Institute
inv.	invoice
IOU	I owe you
IQ	intelligence quotient
IRA	individual retirement account
IRS	Internal Revenue Service
Jct.*	Junction
J.D.	Doctor of Jurisprudence (lawyer)
JP	Justice of the Peace
Jr.*	junior
km	kilometer
kt.	carat, karat
kW	kilowatt
l	liter

lb., lbs.	pound, pounds
L.H.D.	Honorary Doctor of Humanities
LL.B.	Bachelor of Laws
LL.D.	Doctor of Laws
Ltd.*	Limited
Lt. Gov.*	Lieutenant Governor
m	meter
M.A. or A.M.	Master of Arts
M.B.A.	Master of Business Administration
M.D.*	Doctor of Medicine
mdse.	merchandise
memo	memorandum
mfg.	manufacturing
mfr.	manufacturer
Mgr.*	Manager
mi	mile(s)
min.	minute(s)
misc.	miscellaneous
mkt.	market
mm	millimeter
mo.	month
M.S.	Master of Science
Msgr.*	Monsignor
M.S.T.	mountain standard time
Mt.*	Mount
N.*	North
NA	not available
NAM	National Association of Manufacturers
NASA	National Aeronautics and Space Administration
NASDAQ	National Association of Securities Dealers Automated Quotations
Natl.*	National
N.B.	Note well
n.d.	no date
NLRB	National Labor Relations Board
no., nos.	number, numbers
NYSE	New York Stock Exchange
O.D.	Doctor of Optometry
OK	okay
OMB	Office of Management and Budget

OPEC   Organization of Petroleum Exporting Countries
oz   ounce(s)

p., pp.   page, pages
pd.   paid
Phar.D.   Doctor of Pharmacy
Ph.D.   Doctor of Philosophy
Ph.G.   Graduate in Pharmacy
pkg.   package
Pky.*   Parkway
Pl.*   Place
p.p.   parcel post
ppd.   prepaid
pr.   pair(s)
PR   public relations
Pres.*   President
Prof.*   Professor
pro tem   temporarily
P.S.   postscript
P.S.T.   Pacific standard time

qt   quart

Rd.*   Road
R&D   research and development
Re   regarding
recd.   received
REIT   Real Estate Investment Trust
retd.   returned
Rev.*   Reverend
R.F.D.*   rural free delivery
R.N.   Registered Nurse
ROTC   Reserve Officers' Training Corps
RR.*   railroad
RSVP   Please reply.
Rte.*   Route
Rt. Rev.*   Right Reverend
Rt. Rev. Msgr.*   Right Reverend Monsignor
Ry.*   railway

S.*   South
SASE   self-addressed, stamped envelope
SBA   Small Business Administration
SEC   Securities and Exchange Commission

sec.	section; second
Secy.*	Secretary
SOP	standard operating procedure
SOS	radio distress signal
Sq.*	Square
sq. ft.	square feet
Sr.*	Senior
SS	steamship
SSA	Social Security Administration
St.*	Street; Saint
Sta.*	Station
std.	standard
subj.	subject
Supt.*	Superintendent
TBA	to be announced
Treas.*	Treasurer
TVA	Tennessee Valley Authority
U.N.	United Nations
UPI	United Press International
UPS	United Parcel Service
U.S.A.*	United States of America
USA*	United States Army
USAF*	United States Air Force
USMC*	United States Marine Corps
USN*	United States Navy
v. or vs.	versus
VA	Veterans' Administration
Vice Pres.*	Vice President
VIP	very important person
vol., vols.	volume, volumes
W.*	West
WATS	Wide Area Telephone Service
wk.	week
wt.	weight
X	extension (telephone)
xc	Xerox copy
yd	yard
yr.	year
ZIP	zone improvement plan code

Index

A

abbreviations:
  in datelines, 6
  in inside addresses, 10, 165-171
  in legal names, 6
  in letters, 6
  in resumes, 92
  for states, to use with zip codes, 11, 12
  used in business, 165-171
abstract vs. concrete words, 146-147
accept/except, 149
addressing of:
  college and university officials, 163-164
  government officials, 159-162
  lawyers, 9, 164
  military officers, 164
  physicians, 164
  religious leaders, 162-163
affect/effect, 148
agreement of pronoun with antecedent,
  121-122
annual report, corporate, for job-hunting
  information, 83
appearance, professional:
  how to achieve, 3
  importance of, 1, 24
  in sales letters, 71-72

assure/ensure/insure, 148-149
attention line, 11, 13
audience analysis:
  choosing the right audience: 41-42
    for job applications, 81, 105
  importance of, 26-27, 31-32
    in job applications, 82-84, 87
    in letters of persuasion, 57-60, 65-70,
      73, 76-78
awkward compound sentences, 125-126

B

blind carbon copy, 20
Buffalo, City of, 93, 97, 99, 105, 106-107
bullets, in resumes, 104
bureaucratese, 110

C

capital/capitol, 149
carbon copies, 2, 3, 20, 78
carbon copy notation, 20, 43, 44, 45, 75, 78
carbon paper, use of, 2, 20
cardinal numbers, 136
certified mail, 6, 43, 44

Chronicle of Higher Education, 82, 93, 94, 95, 97
cite/site/sight, 150
claim letters, *see* complaint, letter of
clause, 130
cliches, business, 37, 70, 144-46
college and university officials, forms of address, 163-164
company name, in inside address, 10
complaint, letter of, 40-47
    examples, 43, 46
complement/compliment, 150
complimentary close:
    construction of, 17
    placement of, 17
comprise/compose, 151-152
confidential information, treatment of, 25
conjunctions, use in sentences, 125
contractions, use in business prose, 155-156
conversational style, 136-137, 145, 155
cost of a business letter, 25
council/counsel/consul, 152
courtesy titles:
    for men, 8
    for professionals, 8, 159-164
    reasons for omission, 8
    for women, 8
cover letter, with resumes, 94
customer service departments, 41

D

dangling modifiers, 129-131
Dartnell Target Survey, 25
dateline:
    in American correspondence, 5
    arrangement of parts, 5
    importance of, 6
    placement of, 5
    use of cardinal numbers in, 5
deadwood, 114-119
Dick and Jane sentences, 122-124
dictionaries, use of, 2, 114, 138, 150
double-spaced correspondence, 3
dual/duel, 152
Dun and Bradstreet's Million Dollar Directory, 83
duplicating machines, 71-72

E

effect/affect, 148
elite typeface, 1
eminent/imminent, 153
empathy, 25, 45, 49, 51, 54, 56, 105, 146
    (*see also* you attitude)
enclosure line, 19, 43, 53, 64, 97, 107
ensure/insure/assure, 148-149
envelope format, 22-23, 72
Esquire, use of, 9
except/accept, 149
Express Mail, Overnight, 99

F

Ford Motor Company, 40
formally/formerly, 153
form letters, in job applications, 81-82
Fredonia State College, 88, 91, 102
full-block format style, 3, 4

G

gender-based words, 157-158
gobbledygook, 110
government officials, forms of address, 159-162
government regulations, as they affect resume format, 86

H

heading:
    first-page, 3, 5
    second-page, 22, 53, 62, 75
headings, parallel construction of, 132-133

I

imminent/eminent, 153
inside address:
    components of, 7-11
    placement of, 7

insure/ensure/assure, 148-149
interviews, job:
    requests for, 99
    sources of ideas for, 83-84
it, when referring to organizations and
        companies, 121-122

J

Jackson, Tom, *The Perfect Resume*, 84, 86
job application letters:
    examples, 97, 106-107
    importance of references, 98
    purpose, 94
    strategy, 95-99, 105-108
job hunting:
    blind approach, 80-82
    importance of application letter, 94
    informed approach, 82-84
    need to be flexible, 80
    need to establish objectives, 81
    researching the job and company, 82-84
Johnson, Lyndon B., 61
journals, trade, 93

L

lawyers, form of address, 9, 164
layout of resumes, 93
legislators, letters to, 72-78
length of business letters, 32-33
letterhead:
    company, 3, 5
    personal, 5
libraries, uses of, 10, 45, 78, 83, 93

M

margins, 3
military officers, forms of address, 164
mimeograph machines, 71-72
Miss, Mrs., Mr., and M's, 8
Moody's Manuals, 83

N

names, using reader's in body of letter,
        156-157
negative tone:
    in *if clauses*, 29, 98-99
    weak words, avoidance of, 29-30, 51, 54,
        70
numbers:
    rule of ten, 135
    typing of, 135-136
    in vertical lists, 142

O

Occupational Outlook Handbook, 83
onionskin, use of, 2, 20
order letter, 37
ordinal numbers, 136
Overnight Express Mail, 99

P

paper requirements, 2
paragraphs, 138-144
    advantages of short ones, 138-141
    one-sentence, 141-142
parallel structure, 131-135
    in resumes, 132-134
personal/personnel, 153-154
personal and confidential notation:
    placement of:
        on envelope, 22, 41
        on letter, 6
        on sales letter envelope, 72, 99
    purpose, 6, 7, 41
    in job application letters, 99
personal pronoun *I*, use of, 73
    at beginning of sentences, 95
persuasion, letter of, 57-78
    examples, 61-64, 74-75
    underlining words for effect, 137
    use of one-sentence paragraphs in,
        141-142
physicians, form of address, 164

pica typeface, 1
Pinto, 40
positive tone, 28-30, 51, 54
  in letters of persuasion, 70
post office instructions:
  placement of:
    on envelopes, 22-23
    on letters, 6
postscript (P.S.), 21
Prentice-Hall, Inc., 88, 102
prepositional deadwood, 116-117
principal/principle, 154-155
printing methods:
  for resumes, 84, 85
  for sales letters, 71-72
public relations departments, as sources of
  company information, 83

R

reader motives:
  analysis of, 58-60, 65-66
  creation of, 67-70, 76-78, 105
readers' needs, 24-27, 30-31, 33
  in job applications, 81-84, 94-98, 105
  in letters of persuasion, 57-60, 65-70,
    73-78
  in letters of refusal, 48-56
  in letters of request, 34-35, 37
readers' sense of values, 69
redundancy, 114-116
reference initials, 18-19, 46, 53, 55, 64
references, role of, in job applications, 98
refusal, letter of, 48-56
  dual purpose of, 48
  examples, 52-53, 55
registered mail, 6, 44
religious leaders, forms of address, 162-
  163
request, letter of, 34-39
  examples, 36, 38
respectfully/respectively, 155
respectfully yours, as a complimentary
  close, 155, 159

resume, functional, 99-105
  components, 101-104
  education section, 104
  example, 102
  headings, 132-133
  purpose, 100-104
  skills sections, 101-104
  work history section, 104
resume, reverse chronological, 87-94
  activities and awards section, 91-92
  audiences for, 87
  components, 87, 89
  education section, 91
  example, 88
  work history section, 89-90
resume basics, 84-86
  layout, 93
  space-saving shortcuts, 92-93
resumes:
  affect of government regulations on, 86
  definition, 84
  one-page, 85-86
  parallel structure in, 132-134
  printing of, 84, 85
  for teachers and school administrators,
    86
return address:
  on letterhead, 3
  on personal correspondence, 5
rubber stamps, 37, 70, 144-146

S

salary specifications, in job application
  packages, 98
sales letters, 71 (*see also* persuasion, letter
  of)
  printing methods, 71-72
salutation:
  for college and university officials, 163-
    164
  construction of, 14-16
  Dear Sir/Madam:, 16
  for government officials, 159-62
  placement of, 14
  for religious leaders, 162-163

script typeface, 1
sentences, 122-135
    beginning with *I*, 95
    Dick and Jane, 122-125
    short and choppy, 122-124
sentence variety, 122-124
sexist language, 157-158
single-spaced correspondence, 3
site/sight/cite, 150
skills headings, on functional resumes,
    101-103
spacing in letters, 3, 4
*Standard and Poor's Register of Corpora-
    tions*, 83
state abbreviations, 11, 12
stationary/stationery, 155
stenographic notation (see reference ini-
    tials)
strategy:
    direct style, 28, 34-35, 44, 105
    importance of good beginnings, 27-28,
        34-35
    in a job application letter, 95-96,
        105-108
    indirect style, 28, 48-49, 60, 65, 67
    in job applications, 82-84, 87-108
subject lines:
    capitalization in, 13-14
    placement of, 13
    purpose, 13-14
Sullivan, Louis, 61, 99, 106

T

testimonials, in letters of persuasion,
    68-69, 76
that, elimination of, 118-119
this, unclear use of, 120-121
titles, organizational, 9
    placement of:
        in inside address, 9-10
        in signature line, 18
titles, professional:
    placement of:
        in inside address, 8-9
        in signature line, 18

transition words, 143-144
typeface styles, 1, 85
typing requirements, 1, 2, 71-72, 85

U

underlining:
    book, magazine, and newspaper titles,
        137
    words for emphasis, 136-137

V

verbs:
    action, 111-114, 146
    in resumes, 93, 103, 112
vertical lists in letters, 142

W

wasteful couplets, 115
white space, 3, 4, 138, 141, 142
who and *which* words, 117-118
word division at end of line, 137-138
word processor, 72
words:
    choice of, 109-114, 146-156
    commonly confused, 147-155
    economy of, 111-119, 156
    misplaced, 127-129
    sexist, 157-158
    underlining of, 136-137
writing process, three steps of, 1, 2, 109

Y

you attitude, 31-32, 56, 60, 65, 72, 73, 96,
    105 (*see also* empathy)